He Said, She Said

He Said, She Said

Timeless Management Prescriptions

H. William Dettmer

Cover designed and produced by
Lion's Den Studio
East Brunswick, New Jersey
(732) 828-8550

From the Author: I have been as careful as possible to include each quote verbatim and to ensure its accuracy. However, since I wasn't around when most of the quotes were said or written, I can't guarantee everything!

"He Said, She Said - Timeless Management Prescriptions," by H. William Dettmer. ISBN 978-1-62137-564-7 (Softcover); 978-1-62137-565-4 (Hardcover); 978-1-62137-566-1 (eBook).

Library of Congress Control Number: 2014913843.

DEDICATION

For KC

*Without whose invaluable advice this book would not have been as
well organized as it is.
It's never too late to learn . . . and this grasshopper couldn't have had
a better master*

INTRODUCTION

I first encountered the wisdom of humorous modern proverbs (for want of a better description) during my 23 years in the U.S. Air Force. The military is a fertile ground for one-line *bon mots*. One of the earliest ones I can recall came from one of my instructors in pilot training in 1971. When describing the reality of the command structure hierarchy, Captain Thompson said, "Feces do not defy the law of gravity." (S*** rolls downhill.) That observation has been so prevalent over the years that it has finally found its way to an unattributed cartoon that has circulated widely on the Internet for several years:

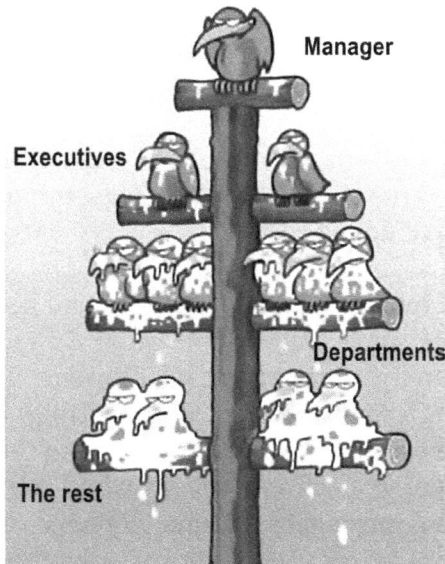

Later, one of my bosses, Colonel Fred Pillet, explained the basic axiom of the air staff officer to me: "An action transferred is an action completed." In other words, if you have an assigned task for which you're responsible that can be shifted to someone else, doing so is the same as completing the task—as far as you're concerned.

Of course, everyone has heard of Murphy's Law: "Anything that *can* go wrong, *will* go wrong." And the corollary to that law is ". . . and it will always happen at the most inopportune time." Then there's also Mrs. Murphy's Law: "And it will always happen when *he's* not home."

Much popular wisdom resides in a sentence or two of accumulated experience. One of the great collections of such wisdom is "The Notebooks of Lazarus Long," an extract from a book entitled *Time Enough for Love*, by the grand master science fiction author, Robert A. Heinlein. Heinlein was renowned for embedding his social and political philosophy in his writing. A typical example:

> *A human being should be able to change a diaper, plan an invasion, butcher a hog, conn a ship, design a building, write a sonnet, balance accounts, build a wall, set a bone, comfort the dying, take orders, give orders, cooperate, act alone, solve equations, analyze a new problem, pitch manure, program a computer, cook a tasty meal, fight efficiently, die gallantly. Specialization is for insects.*

For me, with my education in and natural inclination toward systems thinking, this was the ultimate prescription—and one that I did my utmost to live up to.

By 1989, I had retired from the Air Force and begun teaching graduate courses for the same program in which I'd received my masters degree: the University of Southern California's Master of Science in Systems Management. Shortly after starting that gig, I began collecting quotations such as Heinlein's about human capabilities. Over the years, that collection kept growing. Many were common sayings without an attributable source. Others came from various published sources. One of my favorites originated 500 years ago, with the original master of political and social manipulation, Niccoló Machiavelli:

> *Nothing is more difficult to carry out, nor more doubtful of success, nor more dangerous to handle, than to initiate a new order of things. For the reformer has enemies in all*

those who profit by the old order, and only lukewarm defend-
ers in all those who would profit by the new order, this luke-
warmness arising partly from . . . the incredulity of mankind,
who do not truly believe in anything new until they have had
actual experience in it.

There you have it. The quintessential explanation for why change in organizations is so difficult in the 21st century—from a Renaissance Italian. The more things change, the more they stay the same.

I started collecting these quotations to use in the graduate management courses I was teaching to technical professionals. Within a year, I had 19 pages of such quotations, single-spaced in 10-point type on standard bond paper. Over the next ten years, my collection increased to more than 800 quotations. But in the second ten years I only added another twelve pages. These days, I don't add more than half a dozen quotations a year. Maybe I'm just getting more selective. More likely, it's because I'm seeing fewer new ones that I haven't seen before.

I used pertinent quotations from this collection to begin and end the chapters of several books I wrote in the 1990s and early 2000s, and readers provided positive feedback about them. So, I decided that it's finally time to share with the world what I've collected so far. There's a wealth of wisdom in these quotations—I'd go so far as to say a graduate degree in leadership, management and practical living. My only regret is that I don't have reliable attributions for all of them. Some I have names to attach, but no sources. Some I have sources for, but the quotations that are anonymous were not attributed when I found them. Nevertheless, I hope you'll find something of value in this collected wisdom of others.

H. WILLIAM DETTMER Port
Angeles, Washington, USA
June, 2014

TABLE OF CONTENTS

ACTION

Positive anything is better than negative nothing.
—Elbert Hubbard [7]

A winner makes things happen. A loser lets things happen, or watches things happen and wonders what happened.
—Unknown [7]

An ounce of application is worth a ton of abstraction.
—Booker's Law [4]

He that lives upon hope dies farting.
—Benjamin Franklin [4]

Simple jobs always get put off because there will be time to do them later.
—Dehay's Axiom [1]

You can't build a reputation on what you're *going* to do.
—Henry Ford [2]

Generally speaking, the great achieve their greatness by industry rather than by brilliance.
—Bruce Barton [2]

The bright guys are in cafés discussing how the world should be. Dumb guys are in the office changing the world.
—Felipe Pablo Martinez [2]

Action may not always bring happiness; but there is no happiness without action.
—Benjamin Disraeli [2]

The shortest answer is doing the thing.
                              —Old Proverb [2]

Most of us will never do great things, but we can do small things in a great way.
                              —Not Attributed [2]

Many of us spend half our time wishing for things we could have if we didn't spend half our time wishing.
                              —Alexander Woolcott [2]

To look is one thing. To see what you look at is another. To understand what you see is a third. To learn from what you understand is still something else. But to act on what you learn is all that really matters.
                              —Not Attributed [2]

People who wait until they feel like doing a job rarely do.
                              —Not Attributed [2]

Activity should not be mistaken for accomplishment.
                              —John A. Betti [7]

Vacillating people seldom succeed. They seldom win the solid respect of their fellow men. Successful men and women are very careful in reaching decisions and very persistent and determined in action thereafter.
                              —L.G. Elliott [2]

It is the greatest of all mistakes to do nothing because you can only do a little. Do what you can.
                              —Sidney Smith [2]

Do not wait for extraordinary circumstances to do good; try to use ordinary situations.
                              —Jean Paul Richter [2]

To get anywhere, strike out for somewhere, or you'll get nowhere.
                              —Martha Lupton [2]

No difficult job ever gets done until someone tackles it right now.
—Not attributed [2]

Deliberation is the work of many men; action of one alone.
—Charles de Gaulle [11]

Supervisors are paid to deal with adversity, not just report it.
—Not attributed [2]

The desire to do something good doesn't get it done.
—Not attributed [2]

America needs dreamers who are free to dream big dreams. But we also need "doers" competent to put rivets in those dreams.
—Paul Harvey [2]

Small deeds done are better than great deeds planned.
—Not attributed [2]

Winners outrun defeat by not stopping; losers give in to defeat by not starting.
—Not attributed [2]

Opportunities multiply as they are seized, die when neglected.
—Not attributed [2]

Thunder is good. Thunder is impressive. But it is lightning that does the work.
—Mark Twain [7]

Vision without action is a daydream. Action without vision is a nightmare.
—Japanese proverb [2]

I would rather be a superb meteor, every atom of me in magnificent glow, than a sleepy and permanent planet. The proper function of a man is to live, not to exist. I shall not waste my days in trying to prolong them. I shall use my time.
—Jack London [7]

To stand still is to fall behind.
—Gordon Forward [2]
CEO, Chaparral Steel

The world cares very little about what a man or woman knows: it is what the man or woman is able to do that counts.
—Booker T. Washington [2]

Doing nothing is the most tiresome job in the world, because you can't stop and rest.
—Not attributed [2]

So what do we do? Anything. Something. So long as we just don't sit there. If we screw up, start over. Try something else. If we wait until we've satisfied all the uncertainties, it may be too late.
—Lee Iacocca [2]

Between the great things that we cannot do and the small things we will not do, the danger is that we will do nothing.
—Adolph Monod [2]

People may doubt what you say, but they will always believe what you do.
—Not attributed [2]

Without promotion, something terrible happens—NOTHING!
—P.T. Barnum [2]

An ounce of action is worth a ton of theory.
—Friedrich Engels [2]

Most men lead lives of quiet desperation and go to the grave with the song still in them.
—Henry David Thoreau [2]

The bitterest tears shed over graves are for words left unsaid and deeds undone.
—Harriet Beecher Stowe [2]

To reach a port we must sail—sail, not tie at anchor. Sail, not drift.
—Franklin D. Roosevelt [7]

Do what you can with what you have, where you are.
—Theodore Roosevelt [7]

As I grow older, I pay less attention to what men say. I just watch what they do.
—Andrew Carnegie [20]

Do not let what you cannot do interfere with what you can do.
—John Wooden [20]

CHANGE

Consider how hard it is to change yourself, and you'll understand what little chance you have of trying to change others.
—Jacob M. Braude [2]

Nothing is more difficult to carry out, nor more doubtful of success, nor more dangerous to handle than to initiate a new order of things.
—Niccolò Machiavelli [6]

The only difference between a rut and a grave is their dimensions.
—Ellen Glasgow [7]

The easier it is to do, the harder it is to change.
—Eng's Principle [1]

Any change looks terrible.
—Principle of Design Inertia [1]

Nothing is as temporary as that which is called permanent; nothing is as permanent as that which is called temporary.
—Jose's Axiom [1]

Changing things is central to leadership; changing them before anyone else does is creativeness.
—Jay's First Law of Leadership [1]

It is wise to keep in mind that no success or failure is necessarily final.
—Not attributed [2]

Opposition by others is often proof that you're on the right track.
—Not attributed [2]

Nothing will ever be attempted if all possible objections must be first overcome.
—Samuel Johnson [2]

Established technology tends to persist in the face of new technology.
—Blaauw's Law [4]

There are two ways to meet a difficulty: alter the difficulty or alter yourself to meet it.
—Not attributed [2]

Courage is the power to let go of the familiar.
—Not attributed [2]

The essence of management is recognizing the need for change, then initiating, controlling and directing it, and solving the problems along the way. If it were not so, managers wouldn't be needed—only babysitters.
—H. William Dettmer [7]

Make no mistake: realizing significant improvements in the quality of a product or service . . . is hard, hard work involving a serious amount of grunting and sweating and heavy lifting on the part of all employees. It will mean "doing things better," but it will also mean "doing things differently"—which is to say, it will mean change.
—John Guaspari [2]

If you encounter difficulty, don't change your decision to go. Change your direction to get there.
—Unknown [7]

It is not necessary to change; survival is not mandatory.
—W. Edwards Deming [7]

Failure is not fatal, but failure to change might be.
—John Wooden [7]

Bureaucracy defends the status quo long past the time when the quo has lost its status.
—Laurence J. Peter [11]

All autonomous agencies and authorities, sooner or later, turn into self-perpetuating strongholds of conventional thought and practice.
—Ada Louise Huxtable [11]

Excessive dependence on past policies, however successful, is dangerous in time of rapid change.
—Michael J. Kami [11]

If you want to make enemies, try to change something.
—Woodrow Wilson [11]

Never forget that only dead fish swim with the stream.
—Malcolm Muggeridge [11]

An organization must have some means of combating the process by which people become prisoners of their procedures. The rule book becomes fatter as the ideas become fewer. Almost every well-established organization is a coral reef of procedures that were laid down to achieve some long-forgotten objective.
—John W. Gardner [2]

Beaten paths are for beaten men.
—Eric Johnston [7]

All change is not growth; all movement is not forward.
—Ellen Glasgow [2]

Definition of "insanity": Doing the same thing over and over but expecting a different result.
—Unknown [7]

Change is the end result of all true learning. Change involves three things: First a dissatisfaction with self—a felt void or need; second, a decision to change—to fill the void or need; and third, a conscious dedication to the process of growth and change—the willful act of making the change, doing something.
—Leo Buscaglia [2]

Never doubt the power of a small group of committed people to change the world. That's about the only way it has ever happened in the past.
—Margaret Mead [2]

I have accepted fear as a part of life—specifically the fear of change . . . I have gone ahead despite the pounding in the heart that says: turn back . . .
—Erica Jong [2]

Anything that can be changed will be changed until there is no time left to change anything.
—Arthur Block [1]

It is not the strongest of the species that survive, nor the most intelligent, but the one most responsive to change.
—Charles Darwin [7]

Don't live in the past—you've already been there.
—Not attributed [2]

We can never be really prepared for that which is wholly new. We have to adjust ourselves, and every radical adjustment is a crisis in self-esteem; we undergo a test, we have to prove ourselves. It needs inordinate self-confidence to face drastic change without inner trembling.
—Eric Hoffer [2]

Whenever I see everyone rushing in one direction, I know it's time to move the other way.
—Armand Hammer [2]

People who favor progress, provided they can have it without change, are like those who want a cure, provided they can have it without pain.
—Anthony de Mello [2]

Do not go where the path may lead. Go instead where there is no path and leave a trail.

—Ralph Waldo Emerson [2]

CHARACTER

The best index to a man's character is (a) how he treats people who can't do him any good, and (b) how he treats people who can't fight back.

—Abigail Van Buren [2]

It is what we are that gets across, not what we try to teach.

—Not Attributed [2]

One moment of patience may ward off a great disaster; one moment of impatience may ruin a whole life.

—Not Attributed [2]

Adversity can be a test of character, but most people can stand adversity. If you really want to test their characters, give them power.

—Not attributed [2]

I am tired of hearing about men with the "courage of their convictions." Caligula, Attila, and Hitler all had the courage of their convictions— but not one had the courage to examine his convictions, or to change them, which is the true test of character.

—Sydney Harris [2]

The way a man wins shows much of his character, and the way he loses shows all of it.

—Knute Rockne [7]

What you are shouts so loudly in my ears I cannot hear what you say.

—Ralph Waldo Emerson [7]

Integrity has always determined the difference between winners and losers.

—Tom Peters [7]

What lies behind you and what before you pales insignificant when compared to what lies within you.

—Ralph Waldo Emerson [7]

It's not the qualities you have. It's the qualities you recognize and use that will make the difference.

—Unknown [7]

Most of us fall short of our potential because of little things we know or assume about ourselves. And the most self-defeating assumption of all is that we are just like everyone else.

—Not attributed [2]

Those who cannot believe in themselves cannot believe in anything else. The basis of all integrity and character is whatever faith we have in our own integrity.

—Roy L. Smith [2]

Insincere praise is worse than no praise at all.

—Not attributed [2]

There is nothing so fatal to character as half-finished tasks.

—David Lloyd George [2]

Surveys indicate that certain traits are common to most successful people. These people have a purpose in life, take risks and exercise control, solve problems rather than place blame, care about quality, and share their expertise and knowledge.

—Not attributed [2]

Respect cannot be learned, purchased, or acquired—it can only be earned.

—Not attributed [2]

In order to be a leader, a man must have followers. And to have followers, a man must have their confidence. Hence the supreme quality for a leader is unquestionably integrity. Without it, no real success is possible, no matter whether it is on a section gang, on a football field, in an army, or in an office. If a man's associates find him guilty of phoniness, if they find that he lacks forthright integrity, he will fail. His teachings and actions must square with each other. The first great need, therefore, is integrity and high purpose.

—Dwight D. Eisenhower [2]

One trouble with the world is that so many people who stand up vigorously for their rights fall down miserably on their duties.

—Not attributed [2]

Character is what a person is in the dark.

—Not attributed [2]

If you do not live it, you do not believe it.

—Willie Tyler [2]

Worrying about *what's* right is always more important than worrying about *who's* right.

—Not attributed [2]

The time is always right to do what is right.

—Martin Luther King, Jr. [2]

The height of your accomplishments will equal the depth of your convictions.

—William F. Scolavino [2]

The block of granite that is an obstacle in the path of the weak becomes a stepping stone in the path of the strong.

—Thomas Carlyle [2]

There is no faith which has never yet been broken, except that of a truly faithful dog.

—Konrad Lorenz [2]
Mathematician and meteorologist

Character is that force that enables an individual to carry out a resolution once the mood in which that resolution was born has died.

—Not attributed [2]

I think I began learning long ago that those who are happiest are those who do the most for others.
—Booker T. Washington [2]

Great minds discuss ideas; average minds discuss events; small minds discuss people.
—Admiral Hyman G. Rickover [2]

Hold yourself responsible for a higher standard than anybody else expects of you.
—Henry Ward Beecher [2]

It is not by muscle, speed, or physical dexterity that great things are achieved, but by reflection, force of character, and judgment; in these qualities old age is not only not poorer, but it is even richer.
—Marcus Tullius Cicero [2]

The brave are simply those with vision of what is before them, glory and danger alike, and notwithstanding, go out to meet it.
—Leopold [31]
Kate and Leopold

Patriotism is the last refuge of the scoundrel.
—Samuel Johnson [19]

Be who you are and say what you feel, because those who mind don't matter and those who matter don't mind.
—Dr. Seuss [7]

Weakness of attitude becomes weakness of character.
—Albert Einstein [7]

To know what is right and not to do it is the worst cowardice.
—Confucius [20]

Ability may get you to the top, but it takes character to keep you there.
—John Wooden [20]

COMMITTEES, TEAMS, MEETINGS

Team spirit is what gives so many companies an edge over their competitors.
                                            —George L. Clements [2]

A committee is a form of life with six or more legs and no brain.
                                            —Lazarus Long [3]

A committee is twelve men doing the work of one.
                                            —Kennedy's Comment on
                                            Committees [1]

Those who are unable to learn from past meetings are condemned to repeat them.
                                            —McKernan's Maxim [1]

A meeting is an event at which the minutes are kept and the hours are lost.
                                            —Gourd's Axiom [1]

1. If you want to kill any idea in the world today, get a committee working on it.
2. If you have always done it that way, it's probably wrong.
                                            —Kettering's Laws [4]

My observation is that whenever one person is found adequate to the discharge of a duty by close application thereto, it is worse executed by two persons, and scarcely done at all if three or more are employed therein.
                                            —George Washington [2]

How a committee of five works: one person does all the work, two others tell that person how to do it, a fourth pats the worker on the back for a great job, and the fifth member keeps the minutes of the meeting.
                                            —Not attributed [2]

A meeting is a place where people get together to talk about what they should already be doing.
                                            —Not attributed [2]

If you see a snake, just kill it. Don't appoint a committee on snakes.
                    —H. Ross Perot [2]

A group becomes a team when each member is sure enough of himself and his contribution to praise the skills of the others.
                    —Norman G. Shidle [2]

Group harmony is seldom achieved without personal sacrifice.
                    —Not attributed [2]

A meeting is no substitute for progress.
                    —Not attributed [2]

Creativity always dies a quick death in rooms that house conference tables.
                    —Bruce Herschensohn [11]

In any given meeting, when all is said and done, 90 percent will be said and 10 percent will be done.
                    —Not attributed [2]

Great discoveries and improvements invariably involve the cooperation of many minds.
                    —Alexander Graham Bell [2]

A committee is a group of people who individually can do nothing, but as a group decide that nothing can be done.
                    —Fred Allen [7]

To get something done, a committee should consist of no more than three men, two of whom are absent.
                    —Robert Copeland [7]

A committee can make a decision that is dumber than any of its members.
                    —David Coblitz [7]

A committee is a cul-de-sac down which ideas are lured and then quietly strangled.
                    —Sir Barnett Cocks [7]

Chairing a committee is like taking twelve dogs for a walk.
                            —Marilyn vos Savant [7]

There is one thing all boards have in common, regardless of their legal position. *They do not function.*
                            —Peter Drucker [25]

COMMUNICATION

Many ideas grow better when transplanted into another mind than the one where they sprang up.
                            —Oliver Wendell Holmes [2]

Talking or writing that is too long is generally the result of thinking that wasn't long enough.
                            —Not attributed [2]

The three secrets of public speaking are: be sincere, be brief, and be seated.
                            —Franklin D. Roosevelt [20]

Any simple idea will be worded in the most complicated way.
                            —Malek's Law [1]

The more right you are, the more careful you should be to express your opinion tactfully. The other fellow never likes to be proved wrong.
                            —John Luther [2]

Tact is changing the subject without changing your mind.
                            —Not Attributed [2]

A good supervisor is someone who can understand those not very good at explaining, and explain to those who are not very good at understanding.
                            —Not Attributed [2]

Silence is one of the hardest arguments to refute.
                            —Josh Billings [2]

Anybody can "tell it like it is." What is vastly more difficult is to tell it like it should be.

—Not attributed [2]

Nothing can be said after twenty minutes that amounts to anything.

—Not attributed [2]

The sooner and in more detail you announce bad news, the better.

—White's Chappaquiddick
Theorem [1]

Responsiveness of the firm to the consumer is directly proportionate to the distance on the organization chart from the consumer to the chairman of the board.

—Robert W. Kent [11]

What people don't say is often as important as what they do. When people don't talk to you, they're trying to tell you something.

—Not attributed [2]

The obvious is that which is never seen until someone expresses it simply.

—Kahlil Gibran [2]

Every speaker has a mouth;
An arrangement rather neat.
Sometimes it's filled with wisdom.
Sometimes it's filled with feet.

—Robert Orben [2]

Most conversations are merely monologues delivered in the presence of witnesses.

—Margaret Millar [2]

Tact is the art of convincing people that they know more than you do.

—Raymond Mortimer [2]

Genius is the ability to reduce the complicated to the simple.

—C.W. Cerar [2]

Everything has been said before by someone.

—Alfred North Whitehead [2]
Mathematician and philosopher

If you can't convince them, confuse them.

—Harry S Truman [20]

Speech is conveniently located midway between thought and action, where it often substitutes for both.

—John Andrew Holmes [7]

COMPLEXITY, SIMPLICITY

At some time in the life cycle of virtually every organization, its ability to succeed in spite of itself runs out.

—Brien's First Law [4]

The simpler solution may not be the right one, but it's usually the one to consider first.

—Not attributed [2]

Organizations can grow faster than their brains can manage them in relation to their environment and to their own physiology; when this occurs, they are an endangered species.

—Brontosaurus Principle [4]

One gauge of success is not whether you've solved a tough problem, but whether it is the same problem you had last year.

—Not Attributed [2]

Any intelligent fool can make things bigger and more complex. It takes a touch of genius—and a lot of courage—to move in the opposite direction.

—Albert Einstein [7]

Everything has both intended and unintended consequences. The intended consequences may or may not happen. The unintended consequences *always* do.

—Dee W. Hock [32]
The Sheep's First Law of the Universe

Simple, clear purpose and principles give rise to complex, intelligent behavior. Complex rules and regulations give rise to simple, stupid behavior.

—Dee W. Hock [32]
The Sheep's Second Law of the Universe

Everything *is* its opposite, particularly competition and cooperation. Neither can rise to its highest potential unless seamlessly blended with the other. Either without the other swiftly becomes dangerous and destructive.

—Dee W. Hock [32]
The Sheep's Third Law of the Universe

COMPROMISE

The compromise will always be more expensive than either of the suggestions it is compromising.

—Juhani's Law [1]

A good compromise leaves everybody mad.

—Unknown [7]

Just as most issues are seldom black or white, so are most good solutions neither black or white. Beware of the solution that requires one side to be totally the loser and the other side to be totally the winner. The reason there are two sides to begin with usually is because neither side has all the facts. Therefore, when the wise mediator effects a compromise, he is not acting from political motivation. Rather, he is acting from a deep sense of respect for the whole truth.

—Stephen R. Schwambach [2]

A long dispute means that both parties are wrong.
—Not Attributed [2]

CRITICISM

For every action, there is an equal and opposite criticism.
—Harrison's Postulate [1]

It is ridiculous for any man to criticize the works of another if he has not distinguished himself by his own performance.
—Joseph Addison [37]

A new idea is delicate. It can be killed by a sneer or a yawn; it can be stabbed to death by a quip, and worried to death by a frown on the right man's brow.
—Not Attributed [2]

All my life I've been shot at. Often by the enemy.
—George S. Patton, General, U.S. Army [7]

It is much easier to be critical than to be correct.
—Benjamin Disraeli [2]

Unjust criticism is usually a disguised compliment. It often means that you have aroused jealousy and envy. Remember that no one ever kicks a dead dog.
—Dale Carnegie [2]

It's easy to be critical. The real test is to come up with constructive alternatives.
—Not attributed [2]

After the ship has sunk everyone knows how it might have been saved.
—Italian proverb [2]

Criticism, like rain, should be gentle enough to nourish one's growth without destroying one's roots.
—Not attributed [2]

Criticism isn't nearly as effective as sabotage.

—Charlie Tuna [7]
KCBS Disk Jockey

Criticism is something we can avoid easily—by saying nothing, doing nothing, and being nothing.

—Aristotle [2]

If your number one goal is to make sure that everyone likes and approves of you, then you risk sacrificing your uniqueness and, therefore, your excellence.

—Bob Moawad [2]

Criticism comes easier than craftsmanship.

—Zeuxis (c. 400 B.C.) [2]

When criticized, consider the source.

—Not attributed [2]

When you have no basis for argument, abuse the plaintiff.

—Cicero [7]

DATA AUTOMATION

A computer program does what you tell it to do, not what you want it to do.

—Greer's Third Law [1]

To err is human, but to really foul things up requires a computer.

—Fifth Law of Unreliability [1]

Information technology so far may well have done serious damage to management, because it is so good at getting additional information of the wrong kind.

—Peter Drucker [7]

DECISION MAKING

1. Anyone can make a decision, given enough facts.
2. A good manager can make a decision without enough facts.
3. A perfect manager can operate in perfect ignorance.
> —Spencer's Laws of Data [1]

Good managers learn to share decisions with others even though they alone must accept the responsibility for the results.
> —Not Attributed [2]

There is no more miserable human being than one in whom nothing is habitual but indecision.
> —William James [2]

Decision is a sharp knife that cuts clean and straight; indecision is a dull one that hacks and tears and leaves ragged edges behind it.
> —Gordon Graham [2]

Assume you have absolute authority.
> —Richard Perle [13]

Give your decision, never your reasons. Your decisions may be right; your reasons are sure to be wrong.
> —Lord Mansfield [2]

The larger the number of people involved in a decision, the greater the pressure for conformity.
> —Not attributed [2]

If you want *obedience*, be autocratic and retain full responsibility for yourself. If you want *cooperation*, be democratic and share responsibility. If you want *initiative*, delegate the major share of responsibility and give the person free rein.
> —Auren Uris [2]
> "How to Be a Successful Leader"

When you find people who know their job and are willing to take responsibility, keep out of their way and don't bother them with unne-
cessary supervision. What you may think is cooperation is sometimes
nothing but interference.

—Not attributed [2]

Anybody who makes a real decision after 4:00 in the afternoon should
have his head examined.

—George C. Marshall [11]

If I had to sum up in one word what makes a good manager, I'd say
decisiveness. You can use the fanciest computers to gather the num-
bers, but in the end you have to set a timetable and act.

—Lee Iacocca [2]

The difference between the great and the mediocre is one thing: the
willingness to make a decision. If nothing is happening, you did not
make a decision, you indulged in a fantasy. Action is inherent in any
real decision.

—Danny Cox [2]

The best decision makers are those who are willing to suffer the most
over their decisions but still retain their ability to be decisive.

—M. Scott Peck [2]

Some persons are very decisive when it comes to avoiding decisions.

—Brendan Francis [2]

In a moment of decision, the best thing you can do is the right thing to
do. The worst thing you can do is nothing.

—Theodore Roosevelt [2]

It's easier to ask for forgiveness than it is to get permission.

—Grace Hopper, Admiral, USN [30]

Difficult decisions defy gravity. They travel uphill until they reach the
person at the top.

—Carmen Mariano [2]

It is a characteristic of wisdom not to do desperate things.
                                        —Henry David Thoreau [2]

DELEGATION, AUTONOMY, AUTHORITY

Everybody wants to peel his own banana.
                                        —Young's Principle of
                                          Emergent Individuation [1]

If you have a difficult task, give it to a lazy man—he will find an easier way to do it.
                                        —Hlade's Law [1]

Responsibilities gravitate to the person who can shoulder them; power flows to the one who knows how to use it.
                                        —Not attributed [2]

The most successful executives carefully select understudies. They don't strive to do everything themselves. They train and trust others. This leaves them foot-free, mind-free, with time to think. They have time to receive important callers, pay worthwhile visits. They have time for their families. No matter how able, any employer or executive who insists on running a one-man enterprise courts unhappy circumstances when his powers dwindle.
                                        —B.C. Forbes [2]

The higher you go, the more dependent you become on others.
                                        —Not Attributed [2]

If not controlled, work will flow to the competent man until he submerges.
                                        —Charles Boyle [11]

If you tell people where to go, but not how to get there, you'll be amazed at the results.
                                        —Gen. George S. Patton [11]

Don't tell a man *how* to do a thing. Tell him what you want done, and he'll surprise you with his ingenuity.

—General George S. Patton [2]

You cannot paint the *Mona Lisa* by assigning one dab each to a thousand painters.

—William F. Buckley, Jr. [2]

The best executive is the one who has enough sense to pick good people to do what he wants done, and self-restraint enough to keep from meddling with them while they do it.

—Theodore Roosevelt [7]

DEPENDABILITY, DISCIPLINE

Don't talk about it; just DO it!

—Arthur L. Williams [1]

If you want something done, ask a busy person.

—Not attributed [4]

Make it a point to do something every day that you don't want to do. This is the golden rule for acquiring the habit of doing your duty without pain.

—Mark Twain [2]

Plenty of men can do good work for a spurt with immediate promotion in mind, but for promotion you want a person in whom good work has become a habit.

—Harry L. Doherty [2]

People who have no faith in themselves seldom have faith in others.

—Unknown [2]

Advice from on old carpenter: measure twice and saw once.

—Not Attributed [2]

Don't waste time in doubts and fears; spend yourself in the work before you, well assured that the right performance of this hour's duties will be the best preparation for the hours or ages that follow it.
—Ralph Waldo Emerson [2]

Discipline is the refining fire by which talent becomes ability.
—Roy L. Smith [2]

One worthwhile task carried to a successful conclusion is worth half-a-hundred half-finished tasks.
—B.C. Forbes [2]

A company in which anything goes will ultimately be a company in which nothing goes.
—Not Attributed [2]

Few things are as important as the pride of craftsmanship, at whatever level it may occur—the pride in a job well done, the feeling of having a horse that one can ride.
—Brooke Allen [2]

Management is not being brilliant. Management is being conscientious. Beware the genius manager. Management is doing a very few simple things and doing them well.
—Peter Drucker [2]

In life, just as in football, there's more to winning than just wanting to. You have to give your best every day. You never really lose until you stop trying.
—Mike Ditka [7]
(NFL Hall of Fame TV
commercial)

Take short steps. A lot of people fail because they try to take too big a step too quickly.
—Unknown [7]

There's no such thing as a perfect job. In any position you'll find some duties which, if they aren't onerous immediately, eventually will be. Success depends not merely on how well you do the things you enjoy, but how conscientiously you perform those duties you don't.

—Not attributed [2]

The future is that time when you'll wish you'd done what you aren't doing now.

—Not attributed [2]

An entrepreneur is the kind of person who will work 16 hours a day just to avoid having to work 8 hours a day for someone else.

—Not attributed [2]

Life is a one-way street. No matter how many detours you take, none of them leads back. And once you know and accept that, life becomes much simpler. Because then you know you must do the best you can with what you have and what you are and what you have become.

—Isabel Moore [2]

Failure is the opportunity to begin again more intelligently.

—Henry Ford [20]

The greatest ability is dependability.

—Curt Bergwall [2]

Intentions may be written in pencil; commitments should be carved in stone. Everyone should intend to do the right thing, but commitments should be made only when unconditional, single-minded dedication can be employed. Much disappointment is caused by the confusion of these two words.

—Greg Henry Quinn [2]

The fight is won or lost far away from witnesses—behind the lines, in the gym, and out there on the road, long before I dance under those lights.

—Muhammad Ali [2]

Excellence is not an act but a habit. The things you do the most are the things you will do best.

—Marva Collins [2]

Ordinary people, once they gain the technical knowledge, skills, and competence in understanding how to disarm bombs, have little to fear of them. They are courageous in situations which would cause others great fear. Their fear is dissipated as a result of becoming competent.

—Peter Lowe [2]

You don't aim at the bulls-eye. You aim at the center of the bulls-eye.

—Raymond Berry [2]

I studied the lives of great men and famous women; and I found that the men and women who got to the top were those who did the jobs they had in hand, with everything they had of energy, enthusiasm, and hard work.

—Harry S Truman [2]

It's the little things that make the big things possible. Only close attention to the fine details of any operation makes the operation first-class.

—J. Willard Marriott [2]

I never could have done without the habits of punctuality, order, diligence . . . the determination to concentrate myself on one subject at a time.

—Charles Dickens [2]

DETERMINATION, PERSISTENCE

Nothing in this world can take the place of persistence. Talent will not; nothing is more common than unsuccessful men with talent. Genius will not; unrewarded genius is almost a proverb. Education will not; the world is full of educated derelicts. Persistence and determination alone are omnipotent. The slogan "press on" has solved and always will solve the problems of the human race.

—Calvin Coolidge [2]

Success in business does not depend upon genius. Any young people of ordinary intelligence who are normally sound and not afraid to work should succeed in spite of obstacles and handicaps if they play the game fairly and keep everlastingly at it.
—J.C. Penney [2]

Success is getting up just one more time than you fall down.
—Not attributed [2]

Ninety percent of the work in this country is done by people who don't feel well.
—Theodore Roosevelt [2]

Those who have done nothing are usually sure nothing can be done.
—Not attributed [2]

Nothing is so fatiguing as the eternal hanging on of an uncompleted task.
—William James [2]

You've got to kiss a lot of frogs to find a prince.
—Arthur L. Fry [7]

I have not failed 10,000 times. I have successfully found 10,000 ways that will not work.
—Thomas Edison [7]
(After trying an experiment 10,000 times)

Failure is the line of least persistence.
—Unknown [7]

No one ever created a great thing suddenly.
—John Wanamaker [2]

Failure is the opportunity to begin again more intelligently.
—Henry Ford [20]

If you plant a tree, don't keep pulling it up by the roots to see how it's growing.
                                        —Not attributed [2]

Obstacles are those frightful things you see when you take your eye off the goal.
                                        —Hannah More [2]

The hardest thing about milking cows is that they never stay milked.
                                        —Anonymous farmer [2]

Champions aren't made in the gyms. Champions are made from something they have deep inside them—a desire, a dream, a vision. They have to have last-minute stamina, they have to be a little faster, they have to have the skill, and the will. But the will must be stronger than the skill.
                                        —Muhammad Ali [2]

There are no secrets to success. Don't waste time looking for them. Success is the result of perfection, hard work, learning from failure, loyalty to those for whom you work, and persistence.
                                        —Gen. Colin Powell, USA (Ret.) [2]

A champion is the one who gets up . . . even when he can't.
                                        —Jack Dempsey [2]

My strength lies solely in my tenacity.
                                        —Louis Pasteur [2]

When all else fails . . . use persistence.
                                        —Not attributed [2]

Obstacles cannot crush me; every obstacle yields to stern resolve.
                                        —Leonardo da Vinci [2]

Determination is more important than talent.
                                        —Not attributed [2]

Success seems to be largely a matter of hanging on after others have let go.

—William Feather [2]

The first time you quit, it's hard. The second time, it gets easier. The third time, you don't even have to think about it.

—Paul "Bear" Bryant [2]

Life is not a sprint. It's not even a marathon. It's a triathlon.

—H. William Dettmer

The difference between a successful person and others is not a lack of strength, not a lack of knowledge, but rather a lack of will.

—Vince Lombardi [20]

EFFICIENCY, EFFECTIVENESS

Effectiveness is doing the RIGHT things; efficiency is doing things RIGHT. Productivity is doing the RIGHT things RIGHT.

—Peter Drucker [7]

Bureaucracy is when the first person who answers the phone can't help you.

—Not attributed [2]

Perseverance is not a long race; it is many short races, one after the other.

—Walter Elliott [2]

You can be doing the best job in the world for your client, but if there's something missing, if the client is unhappy, then all your opinions about your performance are worthless. Great service is a matter of perception. Great service is what the client thinks it is.

—Mark H. McCormack [2]

Forewarned, forearmed; to be prepared is half the victory.

—Miguel de Cervantes [2]

It's not the time it takes to take the takes that takes the time; it's the time it takes between the takes that takes the time.

—Steven Spielberg [7]

The difference between efficiency and effectiveness is the difference between knowledge and wisdom.

—Russell Ackoff [27]

EXCUSES

The world is not interested in the storms you encountered, but did you bring in the ship?

—William McFee [7]

If an excuse is good enough, we call it a reason.

—Not attributed [2]

Almost all of our faults are more pardonable than the methods we think up to hide them.

—Not attributed [2]

Most people would learn from their mistakes if they weren't so busy denying they made them.

—Not attributed [2]

A poor workman always finds fault with his tools. (COROLLARY: It's not the sword; it's the swordsman.)

—Not Attributed [2]

Only the mediocre are at their best at all times.

—Not attributed [2]

Stop complaining about what you don't have and use what you've got.

—Not attributed [2]

TOP 10 EXCUSES

1. I thought it was in the mail.
2. I'm so busy I haven't gotten around to it.
3. I didn't know you were in a hurry for it.
4. You'll have to wait until the supervisor returns.
5. I'm waiting for an OK.
6. That's their job—not mine.
7. No one told me to go ahead.
8. That's not my department.
9. That's the way it's always done here.
10. Just as soon as it clears the review board, we'll process your application.

—Laurence J. Peter [2]

Nothing will ever be attempted if all possible objections must first be overcome.

—Samuel Johnson [19]

Man must cease attributing his problems to his environment and learn again to exercise his will—his personal responsibility.

—Albert Schweitzer [20]

Don't find fault. Find a remedy.

—Henry Ford [20]

EXPERIENCE

Experience, however painful, however hard-earned, is a gift. You are entitled to your experiences, because what they are is what you are.

—Unknown [7]

Experience is the ghastly process of trial and error.

—Unknown [7]

Experience is the name everyone gives to their mistakes.

—Oscar Wilde [2]

I am grateful for all my problems. As each of them was overcome I became stronger and more able to meet those yet to come. I grew in all my difficulties.

—J.C. Penney [2]

In time, as one comes to benefit from experience, one learns that things will turn out neither as well as one hoped nor as badly as one feared.

—Jerome S. Bruner [2]

Experience is not what happens to you; it is what you do with what happens to you.

—Aldous Huxley [2]

The major difference between rats and people is that rats learn from experience.

—B.F. Skinner [7]

Experience is knowing a lot of things you shouldn't do.

—William S. Knudsen [2]

There is no such thing as instant experience.

—Oppenheimer's Law [1]

Success is to be measured not so much by the position that one has reached in life as by the obstacles that one has overcome while trying to succeed.

—Booker T. Washington [2]

There's nothing like a little experience to upset a theory.

—Not attributed [2]

Good people are good because they've come to wisdom through failure. We get very little wisdom from success, you know.

—William Saroyan [2]

Experience is the hardest kind of teacher. It gives you the test first and the lesson afterward.

—Not Attributed [2]

The young man knows the rules, but the old man knows the exceptions.

—Oliver Wendell Holmes [2]

A wise person learns by the experiences of others. An ordinary person learns by his or her own experience. A fool learns by nobody's experience.

—Not attributed [2]

Practice is the only way that you will ever come to understand what the Way of the warrior is about . . . Words can only bring you to the foot of the path.

—Miyamoto Musashi [26]

Practice day and night until sword becomes no-sword, intention becomes no-intention.

—Miyamoto Musashi [26]

EXPERTISE, KNOWLEDGE, INFORMATION

The truth of a proposition has nothing to do with its credibility. And vice versa.

—Lazarus Long [3]

Facts do not cease to exist because they are ignored.

—Aldous Huxley [7]

Expertise from one field does not carry over into other fields. But experts often think so. The narrower their fields of knowledge, the more likely they are to think so.

—Lazarus Long [3]

An expert is a person who avoids the small errors as he sweeps on to the grand fallacy.

—Benjamin Stolberg [7]

An expert is that person who is most surprised by the latest evidence to the contrary.

—De Jesus's Observation [1]

To spot an expert, pick the one who predicts the job will take the longest and cost the most.

—Warren's Rule [1]

An expert is one who knows more and more about less and less until eventually he knows everything about nothing.

—Weber's Definition [1]

An expert is a man who has made all the mistakes which can be made in a very narrow field.

—Niels Bohr [2]

An expert is a guy from out of town, with slides.

—Unknown [7]

Repetition does not establish validity.

—Souder's Law [1]

The person with the least expertise has the most opinions.

—Gioia's Theory [1]

If you can't stand the answer, don't ask the question.

—Unknown [7]

The fact that you do not know the answer does not mean that someone else does.

—Steiner's Maxim [1]

Information flows efficiently through organizations, except that bad news encounters high impedance in flowing upward.

—Gray's Law of Bilateral
Asymmetry in Networks [4]

Nobody really knows what is going on anywhere within the organization.

—Johnson's Corollary to Heller's
Law [1]

The greatest tragedy of science is that you often slay a beautiful hypothesis with an ugly fact.

—Thomas Huxley [7]

Enthusiasm without knowledge is like running in the dark.

—Not Attributed [2]

An authority is a person who can tell you more about something than you really care to know.

—Not Attributed [2]

Bad news is the only kind that will do you any good.

—John Boyd [36]

It isn't what you know that counts, it's what you can think of in time.

—Not attributed [2]

When both logic and intuition agree, you are always right.

—Not attributed [2]

Consumers are statistics. Customers are people. Never forget the difference.

—Stanley Marcus [2]

The trouble with the world is that the stupid are cocksure and the intelligent are full of doubt.

—Bertrand Russell [2]

They say it's smart not to believe more than half of what you hear. But which half?

—Not attributed [2]

Beware of half-truths; you may have gotten the wrong half.

—Not attributed [2]

It's a wonderful feeling when you discover some logic to substantiate your beliefs.

—Not attributed [2]

A man is never astonished that he doesn't know what another does, but he is surprised at the gross ignorance of the other in not knowing what he does.
—Haliburton [2]

The greatest obstacle to discovering the shape of the earth, the continents, and the ocean was not ignorance but the illusion of knowledge.
—Daniel J. Boorstin [7]

We are drowning in information but starved for knowledge.
—James Naisbitt [2]

You do not merely want to be considered just the best of the best. You want to be considered the only one who does what you do.
—Jerry Garcia [2]

My greatest strength as a consultant is to be ignorant and ask a few questions.
—Peter Drucker [2]

It is much harder to ask the right question than it is to find the right answer to the wrong question.
—E.E. Morrison [2]

Common sense is genius dressed up in its working clothes.
—Ralph Waldo Emerson

History is a vast early warning system.
—Norman Cousins [2]

Statistics . . . the only science that enables different experts using the same figures to draw different conclusions.
—Evan Esar

Where facts are few, experts are many.
—Donald R. Gannon [7]

I am certain there is too much certainty in the world.
—Michael Crichton [7]

Having all the information is not the same thing as having all the answers.
                                          —Unknown [7]

FOCUS

It is more important to know where you are going than to get there quickly. Do not mistake activity for achievement.
                                          —Mabel Newcomber [7]

You must keep your mind on the objective, not on the obstacle.
                                          —William Randolph Hearst [2]

Doubt as to where or what the goal is—or how to reach it—inevitably leads to confusion and aimless effort. The way a leader goes about setting up objectives for his people has a profound effect on attitude and motivation. If a goal can be made desirable and challenging, the group will drive itself to the utmost to attain it. Confused and unclear goals breed apathy and disinterest.
                                          —Not attributed [2]

We all live under the same sky, but we don't all have the same horizon.
                                          —Konrad Adenauer [2]

If you don't know where you are going, every road will get you nowhere.
                                          —Henry Kissinger [2]

By losing your goal, you have lost your way.
                                          —Friedrich Nietzsche [2]

If we don't change direction soon, we'll end up where we're going.
                                          —Professor Irwin Corey [7]

HONOR, COURAGE

We ourselves impart to our jobs the only honor and dignity they can have. There is no such thing as menial work. There is only menial spirit.
                                          —Alexander Woolcott [7]

Courage is resistance to fear, mastery of fear, not absence of fear.
                    —Mark Twain [2]

Courage is doing what you're afraid to do. There can be no courage unless you're scared.
                    —Eddie Rickenbacker [2]

The question should never be *who* is right, but *what* is right.
                    —Glenn Gardner [2]

There are too many people praying for mountains of difficulty to be removed, when what they really need is courage to climb them.
                    —Not attributed [2]

A man does what he must—in spite of personal consequences, in spite of obstacles and dangers and pressures—and that is the basis of all human morality.
                    —John F. Kennedy [20]

HUBRIS, PRIDE

The greatest of all faults is to be conscious of none.
                    —Thomas Carlyle [2]

People who will not admit they've been wrong love themselves more than they love the truth.
                    —Not attributed [2]

The people most preoccupied with titles and status are usually the least deserving of them.
                    —Not Attributed [2]

Few things make us feel better than having our judgment vindicated.
                    —Not Attributed [2]

It is more practicable to aim to become a department head in three years than to set your heart on the presidency of the company in twenty years.
                    —William Feather [2]

People who admit they're wrong get a lot farther than people who prove they're right.
—Beryl Pfizer [2]

If you go through life convinced that your way is always best, all the new ideas in the world will pass you by.
—Akio Morita, Chairman, Sony Corporation
Made in Japan, (Autobiography) 1986

Don't worry about swallowing your pride. It has no cholesterol.
—Not attributed [2]

No boss will keep an employee who is right all the time.
—The Pitfalls of Genius [1]

What, sir, you would make a ship sail against the wind and currents by lighting a bonfire under her decks? I pray you excuse me. I have no time to listen to such nonsense.
—Napoleon Bonaparte [2]
(to Robert Fulton, inventor of the steamboat)

People work for self-expression. Even when they talk the loudest about "getting the money" they are really most interested in doing a job well so that others will admire it and give them the inward glow of satisfaction which comes of achievement. From the fine artist, producing his masterpieces, to the truck driver, piloting his leviathan across the road, the basic inward thought is—"I am the best . . ."
—H.V. O'Brien [2]

The difference between a general practitioner and a specialist is that one treats what you have, the other thinks you have what he treats.
—Not attributed [2]

The greatest of faults, I should say, is to be conscious of none.
—Thomas Carlyle [2]

Men who succeed at an enterprise of great moment often tie a snare for themselves by assuming that they have discovered some universal truth.
—Neil Sheehan [16]

Don't accept your dog's admiration as conclusive evidence that you are wonderful.
—Ann Landers [2]

The first principle is that you must not fool yourself—and you are the easiest person to fool.
—Richard Feynman [2]

Glory is fleeting, but obscurity is forever.
—Napoleon Bonaparte [2]

The only person more obnoxious than a wise guy is a wise guy who turns out to be right.
—Not attributed [2]

Those who live by the sword get shot by those who don't.
—Not attributed [7]

HUMOR

The organization of any bureaucracy is very much like a septic tank—the really big chunks always rise to the top.
—Imhoff's Law [4]

An optimist goes to the window every morning and says, "Good morning, God!" A pessimist goes to the window and says, "Good God! Morning!"
—Not attributed [2]

If you mess with a thing long enough, you'll break it. COROLLARY: If it ain't broke, don't fix it.
—Schmidt's Law [1]

Authority tends to assign jobs to those least able to do them.
—Cornuelle's Law [1]

Some people manage by the book, even though they don't know who wrote the book, or even what book.

    —Loftus's Law [1]

Anyone who is popular is bound to be despised.

    —Berra's Second Law [1]

Whatever hits the fan will not be evenly distributed.

    —Law of Probable Dispersal [1]

You can make it foolproof, but you can't make it damnfoolproof.

    —Naeser's Law [1]

Teamwork is essential . . . it allows you to blame someone else.

    —Finagle's Eighth Rule [1]

The six phases of a project:

1. Enthusiasm
2. Disillusionment
3. Panic
4. Search for the guilty
5. Punishment of the innocent
6. Praise, honors, and distinction for the non-participants.

    —Unknown [7]

You never know who's right, but you always know who's in charge.

    —Whistler's Law [1]

Never do anything you wouldn't be caught dead doing.

    —Rockefeller's Law [1]

After things have gone from bad to worse, the cycle will repeat itself.

    —Farnsdick's Corollary [1]

Asking dumb questions is easier than correcting dumb mistakes.

    —Launegayer's Observation [1]

There are two things on earth that are universal: hydrogen and stupidity.

—Zappa's Law [1]

Every organization has an allotted number of positions to be filled by misfits. COROLLARY: Once a misfit leaves, another will be recruited.

—Owen's Theory of Organizational
Deviance [1]

Henceforth and forevermore, lawyers shall make more business for lawyers.

—Jim Berry ("Berry's World") [7]

No one is ever completely useless; even the worst of us can serve as a bad example.

—Unknown [7]

1. When in doubt, mumble.
2. When in trouble, delegate.
3. When in charge, ponder.

—Boren's Laws of the Bureaucracy [4]

If a thing is done wrong often enough, it becomes right. COROLLARY: Volume is a defense to error.

—Leahy's Law [4]

No matter where you stand, no matter how far or fast you flee, when it hits the fan, as much as possible will be propelled in your direction, and almost none will be returned to the source.

—Ledge's Law of Fans [4]

Psychologists say there is a definite relationship between pleasure and pain; witness the fact that "golf" spelled backwards is "flog."

—Unknown [7]

Some people who slap you on the back are trying to help you swallow what they just told you.

—Not Attributed [2]

There are three kinds of business people: successful, unsuccessful, and those who give seminars telling the second group how the first group did it.

—Not Attributed [2]

Anytime you want to demonstrate something, the number of faults is proportionate to the number of observers.

—Not Attributed [2]

You can figure you're on the right track if it's uphill.

—Not attributed [2]

Death before initiative.

—Marine Lieutenant's Axiom [7]

Humor is the K-Y® Jelly of the mind.

—Unknown [7]

Everything is funny as long as it is happening to somebody else.

—Will Rogers [2]

To err is human; to blame it on somebody else is even more human.

—Not attributed [2]

Here lies Jack Williams. He done his damndest. What else can a person do?

—Epitaph on a headstone, Boot Hill
Cemetery
Tombstone, Arizona [7]

The higher a monkey climbs, the more you can see of his ass.

—"Vinegar Joe" Stillwell [7]

Even if you win the rat race, you're still a rat.

—Not attributed [2]

If at first you don't succeed, destroy all evidence that shows you tried.

—Fahnestock's Rule for Failure [1]

People specialize in their area of greatest weakness.
                              —The Lippman Dilemma [1]

The time it takes to rectify a situation is inversely proportional to the time it took to do the damage. EXAMPLE: It takes longer to glue a vase together than to break one.
                              —Drazen's Law of Restitution [1]

You can fool all of the people some of the time, and some of the people all of the time, but you can't fool MOM.
                              —Captain Penny's Law [1]

If you wait, it will go away, having done its damage. If it was bad, it'll be back.
                              —Hellrung, Shavelson, Grelb, et. al. [1]

If you leave the room, you're elected. COROLLARY: If you fail to attend, you're elected.
                              —Matilda's Law of Subcommittee
                              Formation [1]

Never sleep with anyone crazier than yourself.
                              —Hartley's Second Law [1]

Everybody is somebody else's weirdo.
                              —Dykstra's Law [1]

Blessed is the man who, having nothing to say, abstains from giving in words evidence of the fact.
                              —George Eliot [2]

You may fight to the death for something in which you truly believe, but keep such commitments to a bare minimum.
                              —Albert A. Grant [11]

Before you criticize someone, walk a mile in his shoes. Then when you do criticize that person, you'll be a mile away and have his shoes!
                              —Unknown [2]

Spare no expense to make everything as economical as possible.
                              —Samuel Goldwyn [7]

We shall reach greater and greater platitudes of achievement.
                              —Richard J. Daley [7]
                              (Mayor of Chicago)

Money isn't everything, but it ranks right up there with oxygen.
                              —Zig Ziglar [2]

The secret to life is honesty and fair dealing. If you can fake that, you've got it made!
                              —Groucho Marx [2]

Man doesn't live by bread alone. He needs buttering up once in a while.
                              —Robert H. Henry [2]

The first rule to tinkering is to save all the parts.
                              —Paul Erlich [2]

To be an actor, you've got to be honest. If you can fake that, you've got it made.
                              —George Burns [2]

If you don't know where you're going, when you get there you'll be lost.
                              —Yogi Berra [2]

All I did was keep turning left.
                                        —George Robson, race car driver [2]
                                        (On how he won the Indianapolis
                                        500)

Baseball is 90 percent mental. The other half is physical.
                              —Yogi Berra [2]

A vacation is what you take when you can no longer take what you've been taking.
                              —Earl Wilson [2]

I guess it's a lot like being in a motorcycle gang—except your mother's still proud of you.

> —Navy pilot on what it was like to spend so many years in an F-14 fighter squadron [2]

The creditor hath a better memory than the debtor.

> —James Howell [2]

Money doesn't make you happy, but it quiets the nerves.

> —Sean O'Casey [2]
> Playwright

People can be divided into three groups:

1. Those who make things happen,
2. Those who watch things happen, and
3. Those who wonder what's happening.

> —Not attributed [2]

Have you seen them? Which way did they go? I must be after them, for *I* am their leader!

> —Not attributed [2]

I can handle pain . . . unless it hurts.

> —Not attributed [2]

LESSONS FROM A CAREER

1. Seek brilliance in the basics, always do the right thing, and have a plan to kill everyone you meet.
2. If you are riding at the head of the herd, look back every now and then and make sure it is still there.
3. Never enter an hour-long firefight with five minutes of ammo.
4. This one is really important for all of you born north of Washington, D.C.—Never, *never* kick a cow chip on a hot day.
5. If you're not shooting, you'd better be communicating or reloading for another Marine.

6. There are three types of leaders. Those who learn from reading, those who learn from observation, and those who still have to touch the electric fence to get the message.
7. Anything worth shooting is worth shooting twice. Ammo is cheap.
8. And finally—you might want to write this one down—never slap a grown man who has a mouth full of chewing tobacco.

> —James M. "Mike" Lowe, Colonel,
> USMC [33]
> Base Commander

When the shit hits the fan, get a tent.

> —William Shakespeare [7]

> NOTE: We all know Shakespeare didn't say this. At least, not the Shakespeare we all know. This came from the Internet. What can you expect . . . ?

IGNORANCE

Man will occasionally stumble over the truth, but most of the time he will pick himself up and continue on.

> —Churchill's Commentary on Man [1]

La madre degli fessi e sempre incinta. (The mother of idiots is always pregnant)

> —Italian proverb [7]

It's the same with narrow-minded people as it is with narrow-necked bottles: the less they have in them, the more noise they make in pouring it out.

> —Alexander Pope [2]

You can say one thing for ignorance: it certainly causes a lot of interesting arguments.

> —Not attributed [2]

No matter how often a lie is shown to be false, there will remain a percentage of people who believe it true.

> —Law of the Lie [1]

A desk is a dangerous place from which to view the world.
—John Le Carré [2]

There is nothing wrong with having nothing to say—unless you insist on saying it.
—Not attributed [2]

Never ascribe to malice what can be perfectly well explained by stupidity.
—Not attributed [2]

A word to the wise is sufficient. A word to the unwise is resented.
—Not attributed [2]

Genius has limits; stupidity does not.
—Not Attributed [2]

Who is it that darkeneth counsel by words without knowledge?
—Job 38:2

The penalty for ignorance is you get beat up.
—W. Edwards Deming [7]

What you don't know will always hurt you.
—Not attributed [2]

Even a stopped clock is right twice a day. After some years it can boast of a long series of successes.
—Ebner-Eschenbach [2]

Light travels faster than sound. This is why some people appear bright until you hear them speak.
—Not attributed [7]

He who laughs last, thinks slowest.
—Not attributed [7]

I won't insult your intelligence by suggesting that you really believe what you just said.

—William F. Buckley, Jr. [19]

A fanatic is one who can't change his mind and won't change the subject.

—Winston Churchill [20]

Wise men don't need advice. Fools won't take it.

—Benjamin Franklin [20]

Great spirits have always encountered violent opposition from mediocre minds.

—Albert Einstein [7]

INSPIRATION, INNOVATION

Apathy can only be overcome by enthusiasm, and enthusiasm can only be aroused by two things: first, an ideal which takes the imagination by storm, and second, a definite intelligible plan for carrying that ideal into practice.

—Arnold Toynbee [2]

To believe is strong. Doubt cramps energy. Belief is power.

—Not Attributed [2]

There is no market for gloom. You cannot sell it. What the world wants, needs, and will buy is cheer.

—Not Attributed [2]

Keep your fears to yourself; share your courage with others.

—Robert Louis Stevenson [2]

I'm looking for a lot of men with an infinite capacity for not knowing what can't be done.

—Henry Ford [7]

He who innovates will have for his enemies all those who are well off under the existing order of things, and only lukewarm supporters in those who might be better off under the new.

—Niccolò Machiavelli [6]

If you talk to the people who work for you, you'll discover that there is no shortage of creativity or creative people in American business. The shortage is of innovators. All too often, people believe that creativity automatically leads to innovation. It doesn't. Creative people tend to pass the responsibility for getting down to brass tacks to others. They are the bottleneck. They make none of the right kind of effort to help get their ideas a try. The scarce people are the ones who have the know-how, energy, daring, and staying power to implement ideas. Since business is a "get—things-done" institution, creativity without action-oriented follow-through is a barren form of behavior. In a sense, it is irresponsible.

> —Theodore Levitt, Professor of
> Marketing [2]
> Harvard University

We know where most of the creativity, the innovation, the stuff that drives productivity lies. It's in the minds of those closest to the work. It's been there in front of our noses all along while we've been running around, chasing robots and reading books on how to become Japanese—or at least manage like them.

> —John F. Welch, Chairman,
> General Electric [2]

An idea can turn into dust or magic, depending on the talent that rubs against it.

> —William Bernbach [11]

Do just once what others say you can't do, and you will never pay attention to their limitations again.

> —James R. Cook [11]

People are always blaming their circumstances for what they are. I don't believe in circumstances. The people who get on in this world are the people who get up and look for the circumstances they want, and if they can't find them, make them.

> —George Bernard Shaw [11]

Creative thinking may simply mean that there's no particular virtue in doing things the way they have always been done.

> —Rudolph Flesch [11]

A genius is someone who shoots at a target no one else sees and hits it.
                                    —Not attributed [2]

Nothing splendid has ever been achieved except by those who dared believe that something inside them was superior to circumstance.
                                    —Bruce Barton [2]

Never design anything you can already build. Always work in the realm of the not-quite-attainable. Otherwise, you're wasting your time.
                                    —R. Buckminster Fuller [7]

The mediocre teacher tells. The good teacher explains. The superior teacher demonstrates. The great teacher inspires.
                                    —William Arthur Ward [2]

If people never did silly things, nothing intelligent would ever be done.
                                    —Ludwig Wittgenstein [2]
                                    Philosopher (1889-1951)

Discovery consists of looking at the same thing as everyone else and thinking something different.
                                    —Albert Szent-Györgyi [2]
                                    American biochemist (1893-1986)

The future is not shaped by people who don't really believe in the future.
                                    —John W. Gardner [2]

The only weapon against bad ideas is better ideas.
                                    —Not attributed [2]

Originality is unexplored territory. You get there by carrying a canoe— you can't take a taxi.
                                    —Alan Alda [2]

Ideas came to me as they do to all of us. The difference is I took them seriously. I didn't get discouraged that others didn't see what I saw. I had trust and confidence in my perceptions, rather than listening

to dogma and what other people thought. I didn't allow anyone to discourage me—and everyone tried. But life is not a popularity contest.
                              —Jonas Salk [2]

He was a bold man who first ate an oyster.
                              —Jonathan Swift [2]

Research is to see what everybody else has seen, and to think what nobody else has thought.
                              —Albert Szent-Gyorgi [2]
                              Scientist

If you want to get a good idea, get a lot of ideas.
                              —Linus Pauling [2]

The universe is full of magical things patiently waiting for our wits to grow sharper.
                              —Eden Phillpotts [2]

Creativity can solve almost any problem. The creative act, the defeat of habit by originality, overcomes everything.
                              —George Lois [2]

The problem is never how to get new, innovative thoughts into your mind, but how to get old ones out.
                              —Dee Hock [7]
                              Founder of VISA

If you can dream it, you can do it.
                              —Walt Disney [7]

I have learned to use the word *impossible* with the greatest caution.
                              —Wernher von Braun [7]

JUDGMENT

You can go wrong by being too skeptical as readily as by being too trusting.
                              —Lazarus Long [3]

If "everybody knows" such-and-such, then it ain't so, by at least ten thousand to one.

> —Lazarus Long [3]

Never underestimate the power of human stupidity.

> —Lazarus Long [3]

Good judgment comes from experience. Experience comes from bad judgment.

> —Higdon's Law [1]

When all else fails, try the boss's suggestion.

> —Strano's Law [1]

When we are right, we can afford to keep our tempers. When we are wrong, we can't afford not to.

> —Not Attributed [2]

When rejecting the ideas of another, make sure you reject only the idea and not the person.

> —Not attributed [2]

The art of being wise is the art of knowing what to overlook.

> —William James [2]

The hardest thing to learn in life is which bridge to cross and which to burn.

> —David Russell [2]

Groups with guitars are on their way out.

> —Decca Records [2]
> (Reason given for rejecting the Beatles in 1962)

Horse sense is good judgment which keeps horses from betting on people.

> —W. C. Fields [2]

Dogs look up to you; cats look down on you; pigs treat you as an equal.
—Winston Churchill [2]

The people I distrust most are those who want to improve our lives but have only one course of action.
—Frank Herbert [7]

Never interfere with your enemy while he's in the process of destroying himself.
—Napoleon Bonaparte [7]

LEADERSHIP

Good supervision is the art of getting average people to do superior work.
—Not attributed [2]

Good executives never put off till tomorrow what they can get someone else to do today.
—Not attributed [2]

I'm just a plowhand from Arkansas, but I have learned how to hold a team together. How to lift some men up, how to calm down others, until finally they've got one heartbeat together, a team. There's just three things I'd ever say:
- If anything goes bad, I did it.
- If anything goes semi-good, then we did it.
- If anything goes real good, then you did it.
That's all it takes to get people to win football games for you.
—Bear Bryant [2]

One of the fine arts of management is the ability to communicate a sense of urgency to the people who work for you without haranguing and without being unpleasant about it. The best method is by showing a genuine, personal interest in their projects and their jobs, checking on progress, and being quick to help in any way you can. There is no substitute for interest. Be interested and stay interested—from start to finish.
—Not attributed [2]

In every organized activity, a small number of participants will become the oligarchical leaders, and the others will follow.
—Sociology's Iron Law of
Oligarchy [1]

It is better to have a lion at the head of an army of sheep, than a sheep at the head of an army of lions.
—Daniel Defoe [7]

The inefficiency and stupidity of the staff corresponds to the inefficiency and stupidity of the management.
—Post's Managerial Observation [1]

No psychology of handling people really works unless we are genuinely and truly interested in other people. All else is mere trickery and will sooner or later fail.
—Not attributed [2]

A great man shows his greatness by the way he treats little men.
—Thomas Carlyle [2]

Good leaders never set themselves above their followers—except in carrying out their responsibilities.
—Not attributed [2]

In handling other people, there are three feelings that a person must NOT possess: fear, dislike, and contempt. If he is afraid of others, he cannot handle them. Neither can he influence them in his favor if he dislikes or scorns them. He must neither cringe nor sneer. He must have both self-respect and respect for others.
—Herbert N. Casson [2]

Most of us decide what we want, then try to persuade others to want the same thing as badly as we do. Napoleon's secret of leadership: he first determined what his men wanted most, then he did all in his power to help them get it.
—Not attributed [2]

How many families have a merit system to measure one child against another? Why should merit systems in the work place do any more to engender team cooperation?

—W. Edwards Deming [7]

The very essence of all power to influence lies in getting the other person to participate.

—Harry A. Overstreet [2]

We've all come to accept that organizations and managers who aren't cost-conscious and productive won't survive. But in the future, we'll also have to be more flexible, responsive, and smarter. Managers will have to be nurturers and teachers, instead of policemen and watchdogs.

—James Maxmin [2]

A leader who can enlist cooperation and respect, without having to pull rank, has power of the most positive kind.

—Unknown [2]

People, ideas, technology—in that order!

—John R. Boyd [36]

You can judge leaders by the size of the problems they tackle—people nearly always pick a problem their own size, and ignore or leave to others the bigger or smaller ones.

—Anthony Jay [2]

Make other people like themselves a little better and rest assured they'll like you very much.

—Not Attributed [2]

Something else is needed: the sensitivity to understand what other people want and the willingness to give it to them. Worldly success depends on pleasing others. No one is going to win fame, recognition, or advancement just because he thinks he deserves it. Someone else has to think so, too.

—John Luther [2]

Stability is more essential to success than brilliance.
                                        —Richard Lloyd Jones [2]

Leadership, at its highest, consists of getting people to work for you when they are under no obligation to do so.
                                        —Not Attributed [2]

There's no limit to what you can do, if you don't care who gets the credit.
                                        —Harry S Truman [7]

The difference between promising ideas and productive results is a good manager.
                                        —Not Attributed [2]

Reason and judgment are the qualities of a leader.
                                        —Tacitus [2]

Executives with true leadership qualities surround themselves with people who are first-rate and upon whom they can completely rely. Only insecure and incompetent leaders look upon their subordinates as potential competitors.
                                        —Not attributed [2]

The most effective leaders are those who satisfy the psychological needs of their followers.
                                        —David Ogilvy [2]

The wise leader does not make a show of holiness or pass out grades for good performance. That would create a climate of success and failure. Competition and jealousy follow.
                                        —Lao Tzu [9]

If you want high efficiency and productivity, a close cordial relationship with your employees that leads to high morale is necessary. Sometimes it is more important to generate a sense of affinity than anything else and sometimes you must make decisions that are technically irrational. But if you work with people, sometimes logic has to take a back seat to understanding.
                                        —Akio Morita, CEO Sony Corp. [2]

He that cannot obey, cannot command.
　　　　　　　　　　　—Ben Franklin [2]

As a leader, you need courage born of integrity in order to be capable of powerful leadership. To achieve this courage, you must search your heart, and make sure your conscience is clear and your behavior is beyond reproach.
　　　　　　　　　　　—Konosuke Matsushita, Founder of
　　　　　　　　　　　　Panasonic
　　　　　　　　　　　　(From his book, *Velvet Glove, Iron Fist*) [2]

Good leaders take at least a little more than their share of the blame, and a lot less than their share of credit.
　　　　　　　　　　　—Not attributed [2]

All great leaders have possessed the *capacity* of believing in the capabilities and talents of others. Those who are always disdainful of subordinates, who constantly denigrate their work, who always compare their efforts unfavorably with their own will wind up leading no one but themselves.
　　　　　　　　　　　—Not attributed [2]

The truth is that bossiness is, without exception, about the worst way, short of violence, in which to get anything done by others, changed by others, or accepted by others.
　　　　　　　　　　　—Donald A. Laird [2]

The trouble with being a leader today is that you can't be sure whether people are following you or chasing you.
　　　　　　　　　　　—Not attributed [2]

One simple fact of life in organizations today is this: If competent people do not manage situations, then incompetent people will.
　　　　　　　　　　　—William P. Anthony [11]

It takes mature, well-balanced people to be good managers—people who can resist the impulse to be self-important and misuse their authority. The only people who ought to be trusted with management powers are those who sincerely respect the rights and worth of every individual. Little dictators can cause a lot of misery.

—Not attributed [2]

Obviously, people must have knowledge in their fields. But the greatest success and financial reward will go to people who have more: the ability to express their ideas, to assume leadership, to arouse enthusiasm and cooperation—in short, the ability to bring out the best in others.

—Not attributed [2]

Workers want a boss who uses a baton—not a club. They want to be led—not driven.

—Not attributed [2]

No man will make a great leader who wants to do it all himself, or to get all the credit for doing it.

—Andrew Carnegie [2]

The only way leaders can make their values tangible and real to followers is through their behaviors and actions. Employees look to their leaders as role models of how they should behave. And when in doubt, they believe actions over words, without fail.

—John Gardner, *On Leadership* [2]

Leadership is the ability to hide your panic from others.

—Not attributed [2]

When you start, you're a manager, and you worry about stuff. At the end, you become a leader and you worry about people. People aren't everything—they're the only thing.

—Elwood "Pete" Quesada [7]

Leadership cannot really be taught. It can only be learned.

—Harold Geneen [2]

One of the tests of leadership is the ability to recognize a problem before it becomes an emergency.

—Arnold Glasgow [2]

Perhaps once in a hundred years a person may be ruined by excessive praise, but surely once every minute someone dies for lack of it.
—Cecil G. Osborne [2]

Leadership is a matter of intelligence, trustworthiness, humaneness, courage, and sternness.
—Sun Tzu [5]

LEARNING

Learn from the mistakes of others; you can never live long enough to make them all yourself.
—Not attributed [2]

There are three things we can do when we make a mistake. We can resolve that we will never make another, which is fine, but impractical. We can let that mistake make a coward of us, which is foolish. Or we can make up our minds that we will let it be our teacher, and so profit by the experience. Then, if the situation comes our way again, we will know just how to meet it.
—Not Attributed [2]

I hear and I forget. I see and I remember. I do and I understand.
—Confucius [7]

To profit from good advice requires as much wisdom as to give it.
—Not Attributed [2]

The teacher learns far more than the student.
—Unknown [7]

Learning usually passes through three stages. In the beginning you learn the right answers. In the second stage you learn the right questions. In the third and final stage you learn which questions are worth asking.
—Not attributed [2]

To teach is to learn twice.
—Joseph Joubert [2]

To introduce something altogether new would mean to begin all over, to become ignorant again, and to run the old, old risk of failing to learn.

—Isaac Asimov [7]

It's what you learn after you know it all that counts.

—John Wooden [2]

People who have a college education often take it for granted, and they're disappointed when it doesn't substitute for working like hell— that it's no magic carpet. All an education does is open a mind; it doesn't fill an empty one.

—Malcolm Forbes [2]

A smart manager makes a mistake worthwhile by being big enough to admit it, strong enough to correct it, and intelligent enough to profit from the process.

—Not Attributed [2]

Wisdom can only be planted, nurtured, and harvested. It cannot be manufactured.

—Kim Brouwmeester [2]

Managers learn while they teach.

—Not attributed [2]

People will pay more to be entertained than educated.

—Johnnie Carson [2]

Failure is not a crime. Failure to learn from failure is.

—Walter Wriston [2]

In times of drastic change, it is the learners who inherit the future. Those who have finished learning find themselves equipped to live in a world that no longer exists.

—Eric Hoffer [2]

Telling ain't teaching, and listening ain't learning.

—Bob Barkley [2]

Learning is discovering that something is possible.
—J. Krishnamurti [2]

By learning you will teach; by teaching you will learn.
—Latin proverb [2]

Curiosity will conquer fear even more than bravery will.
—James Stephens [2]

Failure is a part of success. There is no such thing as a bed of roses all your life. But failure will never stand in the way of success if you learn from it.
—Hank Aaron [2]

Many people dream of success. To me success can only be achieved through repeated failure and introspection. In fact, success represents one percent of your work, which results from the 99 percent that is called failure.
—Soichiro Honda [2]
Industrialist

Whoso would be a man must be a nonconformist. Nothing is at last sacred but the integrity of the mind.
—Ralph Waldo Emerson [7]

In a world that is constantly changing, there is no one subject or set of subjects that will serve you for the foreseeable future, let alone for the rest of your life. The important skill to acquire now is learning how to learn.
—John Naisbitt [2]

The purpose of obstacles is to instruct, not to obstruct.
—Mark Riesenberg [2]

Patience is the courteous space you give to someone in whose learning you have a vested interest.
—Evan B. Welch [2]

The use of traveling is to regulate imagination by reality, and instead of thinking how things may be, to see them as they are.
—Samuel Johnson [19]

The only thing that interferes with my learning is my education.
—Albert Einstein [22]

Education is what remains after one has forgotten what one has learned in school.
—Albert Einstein [22]

He not only overflowed with learning, he stood in the slop,
—Sidney Smith [22]
(English clergyman, on Thomas Macaulay)

Education is a crutch with which the foolish attack the wise to prove that they are not idiots.
—Karl Kraus [22]
(Austrian essayist)

Education is an admirable thing, but it is well to remember from time to time that nothing worth knowing can be taught.
—Oscar Wilde [22]

Success is a lousy teacher. It seduces smart people into thinking they can't lose.
—Bill Gates [35]

LISTENING, OBSERVING

God gave us two ears, but only one mouth. Some people say that's because He wanted us to spend twice as much time listening as talking. Others claim it's because He knew listening was twice as hard as talking.
—Not attributed [2]

You can observe a lot just by watching.
—Berra's First Law [1]

When you talk, you can only say something that you already know.
When you listen, you may learn what someone else knows.
—Unknown [2]

If I could have only two qualities on which to judge a person's promise,
I would choose curiosity and determination. Only the curious will learn,
and only the resolute will overcome obstacles to learning. Curiosity and
determination—these I regard as more important than a person's I.Q.
—Unidentified president of a major
U.S. corporation [2]

One who learns a thing as a skill cannot easily change.
—W. Edwards Deming [7]

Work under a master. Nothing takes the place of working under a master.
Get a job where there is one, travel with him, watch what he does.
—W. Edwards Deming [7]

The art of conversation is as much the art of listening as it is the ability
to express one's self.
—Not attributed [2]

I use not only all the brains I have, but all I can borrow.
—Woodrow Wilson [2]

Maybe if we did a better job of listening, history wouldn't have to repeat itself.
—Not attributed [2]

MISTAKES

A wrong-doer is often one that has left something undone, not always
he that has done something.
—Marcus Aurelius [7]

We've got them!

—Gen. George A. Custer [8]
(On sighting Indians near the Little
Big Horn River, 25 June 1876)

Only a fool can reproduce another fool's work.
                              —Freivald's Law [1]

Nothing is as inevitable as a mistake whose time has come.
                              —Tussman's Law [1]

Asking dumb questions is easier than correcting dumb mistakes.
                              —Launegayer's Observation [1]

THE SIX MISTAKES OF MAN

1. The delusion that personal gain is made by crushing others.
2. The tendency to worry about things that cannot be changed or corrected.
3. Insisting that a thing is impossible because we cannot accomplish it.
4. Refusing to set aside trivial preferences.
5. Neglecting development and refinement of the mind, and not acquiring the habit of reading and studying.
6. Attempting to compel others to believe and live as they do.
                              —Cicero [2]

If you are patient in one moment of anger, you will escape a hundred days of sorrow.
                              —Chinese Proverb [2]

The best way to convince some people that they are wrong is to let them have their own way.
                              —Not attributed [2]

Mistakes are the usual bridge between inexperience and wisdom.
                              —Phyliss Theroux [2]

Only those who do nothing never make mistakes.
                              —Mikhail Gorbachev [2]

The 50-50-90 rule: Anytime you have a 50-50 chance of getting something right, there's a 90% probability you'll get it wrong.
                              —Not attributed [7]

Failure is simply the opportunity to begin again more intelligently.
—Henry Ford [7]

MOTIVATION

You can buy a man's time; you can buy his physical presence at a given place; you can even buy a measured number of his skilled muscular motions per hour. But you cannot buy his enthusiasm . . . you cannot buy loyalty . . . you cannot buy the devotion of hearts, minds, or souls. You must earn these.
—Clarence Francis [2]

When you're making a success of something, it's nct work. It's a way of life. You enjoy yourself because you're making a contribution to the world.
—Andy Granatelli [2]

Never appeal to a man's "better nature." He may not have one. Invoking his self-interest gives you more leverage.
—Lazarus Long [3]

If the failures of this world could realize how desperate half the present-day geniuses once felt, they would take heart and try again.
—Fay Compton [2]

There is nothing in a Japanese car that wasn't in an American car first. They just did it better. We smother innovation with the merit system.
—W. Edwards Deming [7]

The world is full of willing people: some willing to work, the rest willing to let them.
—Robert Frost [2]

I can live for two months on a good compliment.
—Mark Twain [2]

Nothing can stop the man with the right mental attitude from achieving his goal; nothing on earth can help the man with the wrong mental attitude.
—W.W. Ziege [2]

You can hire people to work for you, but you must win their hearts to have them work with you.

—Not Attributed [2]

A person who can't lead and won't follow makes a dandy roadblock.

—Not Attributed [2]

You've got two choices: my way or the highway.

—Valerie Maxwell [7]

The first essential of doing a job well is the wish to see the job done at all.

—Franklin Delano Roosevelt [2]

Promotion awaits the employee who radiates cheerfulness, not the employee who spreads gloom and dissatisfaction. Doctors tell us that cheerfulness is an invaluable aid to health. Cheerfulness is also an aid to promotion.

—B.C. Forces [2]

As a representative of women, I send a message to them, from the villages of Baluchistan to the universities of Lahore, Paris, and Boston. It is "Yes, you can."

—Benazir Bhutto [2]
Prime Minister of Pakistan

Motivation through the principle of self-interest is the center and core of the art of dealing with people.

—Daniel Starch [2]

People who do only what is required of them are, in a sense, slaves. Those who do more are free.

—Not attributed [2]

I'm so optimistic I'd go after Moby Dick in a row boat and take the tartar sauce with me.

—Unknown [7]

Incentive is the soul of success.

—Unknown [7]

Man is a wanting animal—as soon as one of his needs is satisfied, another appears in its place. This process is unending. It continues from birth to death. Man continuously puts forth effort—works, if you please— to satisfy his needs.

—Douglas MacGregor [2]

There is only one way to get anybody to do anything . . . That is by making the other person *want* to do it. There is no other way.

—Dale Carnegie [2]

Complacency is a blight that saps energy, dulls attitudes, and causes a drain on the brain. The first symptom is satisfaction with things as they are. The second is rejection of things as they might be. "Good enough" becomes today's watchword and tomorrow's standard. Complacency makes people fear the unknown, mistrust the untried, and abhor the new. Like water, complacent people follow the easiest course—downhill. They draw false strength from looking back.

—Not attributed [2]

A company that has fun, where employees lunch with each other, put cartoons on the wall, and celebrate, is spirited, creative, and usually profitable.

—David Baum [2]

If you can't get enthusiastic about your work, it's time to get alarmed— something is wrong. Compete with yourself; set your teeth and dive into the job of breaking your own record. No one keeps up his or her enthusiasm automatically. Enthusiasm must be nourished with new actions, new aspirations, new efforts, new vision. It is your own fault if your enthusiasm is gone; you have failed to feed it. If you want to turn hours into minutes, renew your enthusiasm.

—Papyrus [2]

People want to make a commitment to a purpose, a goal, a vision that is bigger than themselves—big enough to make them stretch and grow until they assume personal responsibility for achieving it.

—John Naisbitt and Patricia
Aburdene [11]

If you think you can, you can. And if you think you can't, you're right.
—Mary Kay Ash [11]

The worst loss of anyone is their loss of enthusiasm.
—Not Attributed [13]

The difference between a successful person and others is not in a lack of strength, not in a lack of knowledge, but rather in a lack of will.
—Not Attributed [13]

Powerlessness is a state of mind. If you THINK you're powerless, you ARE.
—Tom Peters [14]

Can success change the human mechanism so completely between one dawn and another? Can it make one feel taller, more alive, handsomer, uncommonly gifted, and indomitably secure with the certainty that this is the way life will always be? It can and it does.
—Moss Hart [2]

If you go by other people's opinions or predictions, you'll just end up talking yourself out of something. If you're running down the track of life thinking that it's impossible to break life's records, those thoughts have a funny way of sinking into your feet.
—Carl Lewis [2]

To the unwilling, nothing is easy.
—Gaelic proverb [2]

Enthusiasm is at the bottom of all progress. With it, there is accomplishment. Without it there are only alibis.
—Henry Ford [2]

There are two kinds of people who never amount to very much: Those who cannot do what they are told, and those who do nothing else.
—Cyrus H.K. Curtis [2]

Obsession doesn't guarantee success. On the other hand, a lack of obsession does guarantee failure.

—Tom Peters [2]

If I believe I cannot do something, it makes me incapable of doing it. But when I believe I can, then I acquire the ability to do it, even if I did not have the ability in the beginning.

—Mohandas K. Gandhi [2]

It is the greatest shot of adrenaline to be doing what you've wanted to do so badly. You almost feel you could fly without the plane.

—Charles Lindbergh [2]

Striving for excellence motivates you; striving for perfection is demoralizing.

—Harriet Beraiker [2]

The best way to motivate other people to help you fulfill your goals is to help them fulfill their goals.

—Deepak Chopra [2]

There is no use whatever in trying to help people who do not help themselves. You cannot push anyone up a ladder unless he is willing to climb himself.

—Andrew Carnegie [20]

A man who has nothing for which he is willing to fight, nothing he cares about more than his own personal safety, is a miserable creature who has no chance of being free, unless made and kept so by the exertions of better men than himself.

—John Stuart Mill [2]

MULTI-TASKING

To do two things at once is to do neither.

—Publius Syrus [2]

The shortest way to do many things is to do one thing at a time.
                                        —Samuel Smiles [2]
                                        Physician and writer

OPINIONS

It is better to remain silent and be thought a fool, than to open one's mouth and remove all doubt.
                                        —Samuel Johnson [19]

When you're in up to your nose, keep your mouth shut.
                                        —Beauregard's Law [4]

Don't ask the barber whether you need a haircut.
                                        —First Law of Expert Advice [4]

The person who seeks your advice too often is probably looking for praise rather than information.
                                        —Unknown [2]

The difference between a successful career and a mediocre one sometimes consists of leaving about four or five things a day unsaid.
                                        —Not attributed [2]

There's a big difference between advice and help.
                                        —Not Attributed [2]

Two quick ways to disaster are to take nobody's advice and to take everybody's advice.
                                        —Not Attributed [2]

Remember the words of James Russell Lowell: "The foolish and dead alone never change their opinion."
                                        —Maxwell Maltz [2]

There is nothing which we receive with so much reluctance as advice.
                                        —Joseph Addison [11]

If in the last few years you haven't discarded a major opinion or acquired a new one, check your pulse. You may be dead.
                                                —Gelett Burgess [11]

No one is more confusing than someone who gives good advice while setting a bad example.
                                                —Not attributed [2]

Between the semi-educated, who offer simplistic answers to complex questions, and the overeducated, who offer complex answers to simple questions, it is a wonder that any questions get satisfactorily settled at all.
                                                —Sidney J. Harris [2]

In the choice between changing one's mind and proving there's no need to do so, most people get busy on the proof.
                                                —John Kenneth Galbraith [2]

Some minds are like concrete—all mixed up and permanently set.
                                                —Not attributed [2]

A good scare is worth more to a man than good advice.
                                                —Ed Howe [2]

There is no better mirror than an old friend.
                                                —Japanese proverb [2]

It is not the same to talk of bulls as to be in the bullring.
                                                —Spanish Proverb [2]

My idea of an agreeable person is a person who agrees with me.
                                                —Benjamin Disraeli [7]

PAPERWORK

The length of a progress report is inversely proportional to the amount of progress.
                                                —Sweeny's Law [1]

Our customer's paperwork is profit. Our own paperwork is loss.
—Brown's Law of Business
Success [1]

We can lick gravity, but sometimes the paperwork is overwhelming.
—Wernher von Braun [11]

PERSPECTIVE

Minor operations are performed on other people.
—Unknown surgeon [2]

It's easy to be optimistic when things are going your way.
—Not attributed [2]

If there is any one secret of success, it lies in the ability to get the other person's point of view and see things from his angle as well as your own.
—Henry Ford [2]

The simple realization that there are other points of view is the beginning of wisdom. Understanding what they are is a great step. The final test is understanding why they are held.
—Charles M. Campbell [2]

No matter how well you perform your job, a superior will seek to modify the results.
—Aigner's Axiom [1]

If it looks easy, it's tough. If it looks tough, it's damn well impossible.
—Stockmayer's Theorem [1]

The highest reward for a person's toil is not what they get for it, but what they become by it.
—John Ruskin [2]

The farther back you can look, the farther forward you are likely to see.
—Winston Churchill [2]

The organization is like a tree full of monkeys, all on different limbs at different levels. Some monkeys are climbing up, some down. The monkeys on top look down and see a tree full of smiling faces. The monkeys on the bottom look up and see nothing but assholes.
—David Ellis [7]

To some people, I am a kind of Merlin who takes lots of crazy chances, but rarely makes mistakes. I've made some bad ones, but fortunately, the successes have come along fast enough to cover up the mistakes. When you go to bat as many times as I do, you're bound to get a good average.
—Walt Disney [2]

If you owe the bank $100, that's your problem. If you owe the bank $100 million, that's the bank's problem.
—J. Paul Getty [2]

It is much more important to know what sort of a patient has a disease than what sort of a disease a patient has.
—William Osler [2]
Physician

When a man sits with a pretty girl for an hour, it seems like a minute. But let him sit on a hot stove for a minute—and it's longer than any hour. That's relativity.
—Albert Einstein [20]

We don't see things as they are, we see them as *we* are.
—Anaïs Nin [7]

PERSUASION

Most people will agree with you if you'll just keep quiet.
—Unknown [2]

Most people make decisions based on emotional rather than logical reasons. Only after they've decided emotionally, perhaps even unconsciously, do they look for rational support for their decisions. You can often achieve great success by convincing people on emotional grounds, then follow up by giving them the rational justification for that emotional decision.

—H. William Dettmer [7]

We flatter ourselves by claiming to be rational and intellectual beings, but it would be a great mistake to suppose that people are always guided by reason. We are strange, inconsistent creatures, and act quite as often, perhaps oftener, from prejudice or passion. The result is that you are more likely to carry people with you by enlisting their feelings than by convincing their reason.

—John Lubbock [2]

When you can, always advise people to do what you see they really want to do . . . Doing what they want to do, they may succeed; doing what they don't want to do, they won't.

—James Gould Cozzens [2]

There is a mighty big difference between good, sound reasons and reasons that sound good.

—Burton Hillis [2]

You cannot antagonize and persuade at the same time.

—Not Attributed [2]

The shepherd always tries to persuade the sheep that their interests and his own are the same.

—Marie Henri Beyle [2]

Good examples have twice the value of good advice.

—Not Attributed [2]

There are few things more difficult than the art of making advice agreeable.

—Not Attributed [2]

The weaker the argument, the stronger the words.

—Not attributed [2]

I would rather try to persuade a man to go along, because once I have persuaded him, he will stick. If I scare him, he will stay just as long as he is scared, and then he is gone.
　　　　　　　　　　　—Dwight D. Eisenhower [2]

Force has no place where there is need of skill.
　　　　　　　　　　　—Herodotus [11]

A manger, no matter how brilliant, cannot alone achieve acceptance of and support for change from those affected or otherwise involved. To do so, he must depend on others.
　　　　　　　　　　　—Arnold S. Judson [11]

You can fool all of the people all of the time if the advertising is right and the budget is big enough.
　　　　　　　　　　　—Joseph E. Levine [11]

Selling a decision is as important as making a decision. Decision makers must take time to develop selling strategies that turn ideas into action.
　　　　　　　　　　　—Philip Marvin [11]

One should use statistics as a drunk uses a lamp post—for support rather than illumination.
　　　　　　　　　　　—Not attributed [2]

To be persuasive, we must be believable. To be believable, we must be credible. To be credible, we must be truthful.
　　　　　　　　　　　—Edward R. Murrow [2]

Passion persuades.
　　　　　　　　　　　—Anita Roddick [2]

Work underground as long as you can. Publicity triggers the corporate immune system.
　　　　　　　　　　　—Gifford Pinchot, III [7]

You can get a lot farther with a kind word and a gun than you can with a kind word alone.

—Al Capone [2]

If you would persuade, you must appeal to interest rather than intellect.

—Benjamin Franklin [2]

We are generally the better persuaded by the reasons we discover ourselves than by those given to us by others.

—Blaise Pascal [2]

PHILOSOPHY

An optimist believes we live in the best of all possible worlds. A pessimist fears this is true.

—The Cardinal Conundrum [1]

To beat the bureaucracy, make your problem their problem.

—Principle of Displaced Hassle [4]

Speak with authority; however, expound only on the obvious and proven facts.

—Spark's Third Rule for
Managers [1]

The first myth of management is that it exists.

—Heller's Law [1]

Security isn't. Management can't. Sales promotions don't. Consumer assistance doesn't. Workers don't.

—Brooks's Law of Retailing [1]

Nothing is ever so bad that it can't get worse.

—Gattuso's Extension of Murphy's
Law [1]

A fat profit margin encourages rising costs.

—Unknown [2]

The best way to succeed in life is to act on the advice we give to others.
—Unknown [2]

Every great achievement was once IMPOSSIBLE.
—Unknown [2]

Take great care to let nobody discover that you know your own value. Whatever real merit you have, other people will discover, and people always magnify their own discoveries, as they lessen those of others.
—Lord Chesterfield [2]

The only thing free in America is a screwing.
—Arthur L. Williams [7]

Victories that come cheap, are cheap. Those only are worth having which come as a result of hard fighting.
—Henry Ward Beecher [2]

Competition should be directed toward doing a better job, not toward getting a bigger share of the market. Do the first, and the second will take care of itself.
—W. Edwards Deming [7]

I not only bow to the inevitable, I am fortified by it.
—Thornton Wilder [2]

The essence of intelligence is skill in extracting meaning from everyday experience.
—Unknown [2]

Nothing ever gets built on time or under budget.
—Cheops's Law [4]

No good deed goes unpunished.
—Clare Booth Luce's Law [4]

When a customer buys a low-grade article, he feels pleased when he pays for it and displeased every time he uses it. When he buys a well-made article, he feels extravagant when he pays for it and well pleased every time he uses it.

—Herbert N. Casson [2]

The only way to conquer fear is to keep doing the thing you fear to do.

—Not Attributed [2]

The worst crime against working people is a company that fails to operate at a profit.

—Samuel L. Gompers [2]

The best time to look for work is AFTER you get the job.

—Not Attributed [2]

Forget your opponents; always play against par.

—Sam Snead [2]

The young make the mistake of thinking that education can take the place of experience; the old, that experience can take the place of education.

—Not Attributed [2]

You can never really get away; you can only take yourself somewhere else.

—Not Attributed [2]

We have to have frustrations. You just have to learn how to live with them. Sometimes you win and sometimes you lose, but don't allow yourself to be made a fool of by either success or failure. You have to learn how to rise above both success and failure.

—Robert Frost [2]

If you stand up and be counted, from time to time you may even get yourself knocked down. But remember this: Someone flattened by an opponent can get up. Someone flattened by conformity stays down for good.

—Thomas J. Watson, Jr. [2]

- Mind your own business—and have plenty of it.
- Tackle one job at a time.
- Make decisions quickly, and don't fear the outcome.
- Learn to delegate a part of your work and your responsibilities.
- Don't stake too much on success.
- Don't be afraid of failure.
- Don't overvalue the unattainable.
- Don't undervalue what you have.
- Forget the people you don't like.
- Keep both your senses of humor and proportion.
- Forget yesterday—it's gone.
- Don't dread tomorrow—it isn't here yet.

—Not attributed [2]

The real test of business greatness lies in giving opportunity to others.

—Charles Schwab [2]

Failures are divided into two classes: those who thought and never did, and those who did and never thought.

—Not Attributed [2]

It is in human nature to think wisely and act in an absurd fashion.

—Anatole France [2]

Not a day passes over the earth but men and women of no note do great deeds, speak great words, and suffer noble sorrows.

—Charles Reade [2]

Unused talents give you no advantage whatever over someone who has no talents at all.

—Not attributed [2]

Gravity isn't easy, but it's the law.

—Not attributed [2]

The only things that evolve by themselves in an organization are disorder, friction, and malperformance.

—Peter Drucker [11]

How many managerial roles are required when standards are explicit? Does the need for managers increase in direct proportion to the levels of abstraction at which standards are stated?
—Woodrow H. Sears, Jr. [11]

Great minds have purposes; little minds have wishes. Little minds are subdued by misfortunes; great minds rise above them.
—Washington Irving [2]

There are lots of ways to make employees feel that their jobs are important:

• Talk with them frequently
• Explain the importance of doing this job well
• Give them occasional special responsibilities
• Watch for special abilities; praise good work in front of others
• Ask their opinion about various problems
• Listen to their opinions
• Show an interest in them and their personal lives
—John L. Beckley [2]

The quality of a person's life is in direct proportion to their commitment to excellence, regardless of their chosen field of endeavor.
—Not Attributed [13]

Our conduct is influenced not by our experience but by our expectations.
—George Bernard Shaw [2]

The stupid neither forgive nor forget. The naive forgive and forget. The wise forgive but do not forget.
—Not attributed [2]

See everything, overlook a lot, correct a little.
—Pope John XXIII [2]

Ten "Cannots":

1. You cannot bring about prosperity by discouraging thrift.
2. You cannot help small men by tearing down big men.
3. You cannot strengthen the weak by weakening the strong.
4. You cannot lift the wage earner by pulling down the wage payer.
5. You cannot help the poor man by destroying the rich.
6. You cannot keep out of trouble by spending more than your income.
7. You cannot further the brotherhood of man by inciting class hatred.
8. You cannot establish security on borrowed money.
9. You cannot build character and courage by taking away men's initiative and independence.
10. You cannot help men permanently by doing for them what they could and should do for themselves.

—Rev. William J.H. Boetcker [7]

Policies are many, principles are few. Policies will change, principles never do.

—John C. Maxwell [2]
Developing the Leader Within You

Before the beginning of great brilliance, there must be chaos. Before a brilliant person begins something great, he must look foolish to the crowd.

—*I Ching* [2]

Hard work is simply the accumulation of easy things I didn't do when I should have done them.

—Dr. Dale E. Turner [2]

Management is a set of processes that can keep a complicated system of people and technology running smoothly. The most important aspects of management include planning, budgeting, organizing, staffing, controlling, and problem solving. Leadership is a set of processes that creates organizations in the first place, or adapts them to significantly changing circumstances. Leadership defines what the future should look like, aligns people with that vision, and inspires them to make it happen despite the obstacles.

—John F. Kotter [15]

We can easily forgive a child who is afraid of the dark; the real tragedy of life is when men are afraid of the light.

> —Plato [2]

If you want to reach your goals, you need to change your vocabulary.

> —Unknown [7]

If you treat everybody like they're hurting, you'll be treating the vast majority of them in the proper way.

> —Unknown [7]

The art of nurturing oneself is not taught in most high schools or even in a good MBA course. In fact, the art of nurturing oneself is rarely taught in families either. Yet in this high-tech, high-information society, learning how to nurture oneself is absolutely essential for survival. Nurturing myself is allowing myself to know what would be healing for me right now—and doing it.

> —Unknown [7]

Enthusiasm is like running in the dark. You might get there, but you also might get killed on the way.

> —Unknown [7]

If you want to create a cripple, just give a man a pair of crutches for a few months.

> —Unknown [7]

A small trouble is like a pebble. Hold it too close to your eye and it fills the whole world and puts everything out of focus. Hold it at proper viewing distance and it can be examined and properly classified. Throw it at your feet and it can be seen in its true setting: just one more tiny bump on the pathway to eternity.

> —Celia Luce [2]

What employees have a reasonable right to expect from a job:

1. *Meaningful work*, designed to have elements of reward and satisfaction.
2. *Fair treatment* for all employees.

3. *Accurate appraisal*, and appropriate rewards for superior performance.
4. *Opportunity for advancement*—more responsibility and a commensurate financial reward.
5. *Security*—the feeling that if you do your job, you won't lose it.
6. *Training*—when job requirements change, workers should be helped to meet the company's expectations.
7. *Knowledge of the "system"*—how the pieces of the puzzle fit together, so that employees know how they fit into the system and what they must do to advance within it.
8. *A voice in company affairs*—employees need to feel that someone is willing to listen when they have a contribution or complaint to make.
9. *Pleasant working conditions*—evidence that the company cares about the physical comfort of the employees.
10. *Retirement benefits*—these should come in return for the contribution of the employees to the company over their working years.

—James Leonard, President [2]
First National Bank of Chicago

Never get into a contest with someone who has nothing to lose.
—Unknown [7]

It is useless for the sheep to give speeches in favor of vegetarianism while the wolf remains of a different opinion.
—Unknown [7]

The less work an organization produces, the more frequently it reorganizes.
—Jacobson's Law [1]

They can't hit it while I'm standing here holding it.
—Lefty Gomez's Principle of
Productive Procrastination [1]

There is nothing so small it can't be blown out of proportion.
—Ruckert's Law [1]

Life can only be understood backwards, but it must be lived forwards.
—Kierkegaard's Observation [1]

Trust only those who stand to lose as much as you when things go wrong.
                          —Bralek's Rule for Success [1]

Whoever has the gold makes the rules.
                          —The Golden Rule of Arts and
                          Sciences [1]

Find a need and fill it.
                          —Ruth Stafford Peale [2]

What a father says to his children is not heard by the world, but it will be heard by posterity.
                          —Jean Paul Richter [2]

The harder the conflict, the more glorious the triumph. What we obtain cheap, we esteem too lightly; 'tis dearness only that gives everything its value.
                          —Thomas Paine [2]

You can know a person by the kind of desk he keeps. If the president of a company has a clean desk, then it must be the executive vice president who is doing all the work.
                          —Harold S. Geneen [2]

Lost yesterday, somewhere between sunrise and sunset, two golden hours, each set with 60 diamond-studded minutes. No reward is offered, for they are gone forever.
                          —Horace Mann [2]

There is always free cheese in a mousetrap.
                          —Not attributed [2]

If you come to fork in the road, take it.
                          —Yogi Berra [2]

There is one rule for industrialists and that is: make the best quality of goods possible at the lowest possible cost, paying the highest wages possible.
                          —Henry Ford [2]

I have little patience with scientists who take a board of wood, look for its thinnest part, and drill a great number of holes where drilling is easy.
—Albert Einstein [2]

In my humble opinion, noncooperation with evil is as much a duty as cooperation with good.
—Mohandas K. Gandhi [2]

Heredity is nothing but stored environment.
—Luther Burbank [2]

The two hardest things to handle in life are failure and success.
—Not attributed [2]

Work is of two kinds: First, altering the position of matter at or near the earth's surface relative to other matter. Second, telling other people to do so.
—Bertrand Russell [2]

With every disadvantage, there is always a greater advantage.
—W. Clement Stone [2]

Not everything that can be counted counts, and not everything that counts can be counted.
—Albert Einstein [7]

Your companions are like the buttons on an elevator. They will either take you up or they will take you down.
—Not attributed [2]

The two "Be's" of marketing:

1) Be different to be remembered.
2) Be better to be bought.
—Mike Altshuler [2]

The greatest achievements are those that benefit others.
—Denis Waitley [2]

Adversity is like a strong wind. It tears away from us all but the things that cannot be torn, so that we see ourselves as we really are.
—Arthur Golden [34]

To succeed, it is necessary to accept the world as it is and rise above it.
—Michael Korda [2]

An idealist believes that the short run doesn't count. A cynic believes that the long run doesn't matter. A realist believes that what is done or left undone in the short run determines the long run.
—Sydney J. Harris [2]

You Americans will always do the right thing, after you exhaust all other possibilities.
—Winston Churchill [7]

We have met the enemy, and he is us.
—Walt Kelly [2]

A people that values its privileges above its principles soon loses both.
—Dwight D. Eisenhower [7]

The graveyards are full of indispensable men.
—Charles DeGaulle [20]

Neither a wise man nor a brave man lies down on the tracks of history to wait for the train of the future to run over him.
—Dwight D. Eisenhower [20]

If we could read the secret history of our enemies, we should find in each man's life sorrow and suffering enough to disarm all hostility.
—Henry Wadsworth Longfellow [24]

Life should not be a journey to the grave with the intention of arriving safely in an attractive and well preserved body. But rather to skid in sideways, chocolate in one hand, martini in the other, body thoroughly used up, totally worn out and screaming "WOO-HOO! What a ride!"
—Not attributed [7]

Contrarianism is creativity to the untalented.
                         —Dennis Miller [7]

PLANNING

Lack of planning on your part does not constitute an emergency on my
part.
                         —Unknown [7]

Plans get you into things, but you got to work your own way out.
                         —Will Rogers [7]

Luck: when preparation meets opportunity.
                         —Unknown [7]

Control is the child of planning; crisis management should not be
confused with leadership—it's janitorship.
                         —H. William Dettmer [7]

The white man knows how to make everything, but he does not know
how to distribute it.
                         —Sitting Bull, 1885 [8]

If asked when you can deliver something, ask for time to think. Build
in a margin of safety. Name a date. Then deliver it earlier than you
promised. The world is divided into two classes of people: the few
who make good on their promises (even if they don't promise as
much), and the many who don't. Get into Column "A" and stay there.
You'll be very valuable wherever you are.
                         —Robert Townsend [2]

Everybody sets out to do something, and everybody does something,
but most people don't do what they set out to do.
                         —George Moore [2]

Victory awaits the one who has prepared everything in advance—
people call it luck. Defeat is certain for the one who did not make the
necessary preparations in time—people call it misfortune.
                         —Roald Amundsen [7]

The beginning is the most important part of the work.
—Plato [2]

The great dividing line between success and failure can be stated in five words: *I did not have time*.
—Henry Davenport [2]

Long-range planning does not deal with future decisions, but with the future of present decisions.
—Peter F. Drucker [2]

Failure to prepare is preparing to fail.
—John Wooden [20]

If you don't have your own plan, someone else is going to make you fit into their plan.
—Anthony Robbins [7]

POLITICS

Don't let your superiors know you are better than they are.
—First Rule of Superior
Inferiority [1]

1. No matter what they're telling you, they're not telling you the truth.
2. No matter what they're talking about, they're talking about money.
—Todd's First Two Political
Principles [1]

Attempt to be seen with important people.
—Spark's Second Rule for
Managers [1]

The art of diplomacy is saying, "Nice doggie, nice doggie," until you can find a stick.
—Will Rogers [7]

The most essential qualification for a politician is the ability to fore-tell what will happen tomorrow, next month, and next year—and to ex-plain afterward why it did not happen.

—Winston Churchill [2]

Well, it's probably better to have him inside the tent pissing out than outside pissing in.

—Lyndon B. Johnson (On deciding to
retain J. Edgar Hoover as Director
of the FBI, 1964) [8]

Christmas is a time when children ask Santa Claus for what they want and adults pay for it. Deficits are when adults spend what they want and children pay for it.

—Richard Lamm [2]
(Former Governor of Colorado)

Any 20-year-old who isn't a liberal doesn't have a heart, and any 40-year-old who isn't a conservative doesn't have a brain.

—Winston Churchill [2]

Capitalism's problem is the uneven distribution of wealth, while socialism's virtue is the even distribution of misery.

—Winston Churchill [7]

Govern a great nation as you would cook a small fish. Do not overdo it.

—Lao-Tzu [2]

There are two places where socialism will work: In heaven, where it is not needed, and in Hell, where they already have it.

—Winston Churchill [2]

What will get you promoted on one level will get you killed on another.

—Fox on Levelology [1]

The people to worry about are not those who openly disagree with you, but those who disagree with you and are too cowardly to let you know.

—Not attributed [2]

Giving money and power to government is like giving whiskey and car keys to teenage boys.

—P. J. O'Rourke [7]

"Politics" derives from the Greek word *poly*, meaning *many*, and *tics*, which, as everybody knows, are blood-sucking parasites.

—Unknown [7]

Public money ought to be touched with the most scrupulous conscientiousness of honor. It is not the product of riches only, but of the hard earnings of labor and poverty. It is drawn even from the bitterness of want and misery. Not a beggar passes, or perishes in the streets, whose mite is not in that mass.

—Thomas Paine [7]

Work underground as long as you can. Publicity triggers the corporate immune system.

—Gifford Pinchot, III [7]

Politicians are drawn to cameras like flies are drawn to politicians.

—Unknown

Eternal vigilance is the price of liberty.

—Thomas Jefferson [20]

Forgive your enemies, but never forget their names.

—John F. Kennedy [20]

My choices in life were either to be a piano player in a whore house or a politician. And to tell the truth, there's hardly any difference.

—Harry S Truman [7]

PRIORITIES

No amount of genius can overcome a preoccupation with detail.

—Levy's Eighth Law [1]

One of the characteristics of a workaholic is procrastination. Often, our busyness is a subtle form of procrastination that keeps us away from what we *really* need to be doing.
—Not attributed [7]

A budget is a statement of priorities, and there's no more political a document.
—Edward K. Hamilton [11]

Anything less than a conscious commitment to the important is an unconscious commitment to the unimportant.
—Steven Covey [2]

PROBLEM SOLVING

Complex problems have simple, easy-to-understand wrong answers.
—Grossman's Misquote of H.L. Mencken [2]

Doing things the hard way is always easier.
—Murphy's Paradox [1]

Any technical problem can be overcome, given enough time and money. COROLLARY: You are never given enough time and money.
—Lerman's Law of Technology [1]

If one views his problem closely enough, he will recognize himself as part of the problem.
—Ducharm's Axiom [1]

Anything is easier to take apart than to put together.
—Washlesky's Law [1]

If you take something apart and put it back together enough times, eventually you will have two of them.
—Rap's Law of Inanimate Reproduction [1]

Almost anything is easier to get into than to get out of.
—Allen's Law [1]

If you can't fix it, feature it.
—Last Law of Product Design [1]

Save all the parts.
—First Rule of Intelligent
Tinkering [1]

If things are not going well with you, begin your effort at correcting the situation by carefully examining the service you are rendering, and especially the spirit in which you are rendering it.
—Roger Babson [2]

Average managers are concerned with methods, opinions, and precedents. Good managers are concerned with solving problems.
—Not Attributed [2]

Fix the system, not the blame.
—Myron Tribus [7]

Managers who attack results without analyzing causes usually make matters worse rather than better.
—Not attributed [2]

The surest way to mishandle a problem is to avoid facing up to it.
—Not attributed [2]

Inside every large problem is a small problem struggling to get out.
—Hoare's Law of Large Problems [1]

Look for the *second* right answer.
—Unknown [7]

Accept the challenges so that you may feel the exhilaration of victory.
—Not Attributed [13]

We are all faced with great opportunities . . . brilliantly disguised as impossible situations.

—Not attributed [2]

Never cut what you can untie.

—Joseph Joubert [2]

When you look in the mirror, you are looking at the problem. But remember, you are also looking at the solution.

—Not attributed [2]

Real difficulties can be overcome; it is only the imaginary ones that are unconquerable.

—Theodore N. Vail [2]

Silver bullets disappeared when the Lone Ranger died.

—Ray Hansen [7]

Roadblocks aren't barriers—they open your eyes to other routes.

—Joyce Restaino [2]

QUALITY, IMPROVEMENT

Quality is never an accident; it is always the result of intelligent effort.

—John Ruskin [2]

Quality is inversely proportional to the time left for the completion of the project.

—Wright's First Law of Quality [1]

Total Quality Management is about prevention, not correction. It's easier to prevent poor quality than to correct it.

—John A. Betti
Undersecretary of Defense,
Acquisition [7]

There is no such thing as staying the same. You are either striving to make yourself better or allowing yourself to get worse.

—Unknown [7]

The best way to get relief from a monotonous task is to think up ways of improving it.

—Not Attributed [2]

If you're not working at your game to the utmost of your ability, there will be someone out there somewhere with equal ability who will be working to the utmost of his ability. And one day you'll play each other, and he'll have the advantage.

—"Easy Ed" Macauley [7]

The human race has improved everything except the human race.

—Adlai Stevenson [2]

The real fault is to have faults and not try to mend them.

—Confucius [2]

Everything now being done is going to be done differently; it's going to be done better, and if you don't do it, your competitor will.

—Not Attributed [2]

Once we realize that imperfect understanding is the human condition, there is no shame in being wrong, only in failing to correct our mistakes.

—George Soros [2]

If a man has done his best, what else is there?

—George S. Patton, Jr. [20]

There is scarcely anything in the world that some man cannot make a little worse, and sell a little more cheaply. The person who buys on price alone is this man's lawful prey.

—John Ruskin [23]

There is more leverage for improvement in your own policies than you ever dreamed possible

—Peter Senge [18]

RISK, CONTINGENCY

A memorandum is written not to inform the reader, but to protect the writer.

> —Acheson's Rule of the
> Bureaucracy [4]

There are men so conservative they believe nothing should be done for the first time.

> —Unknown [7]

What we anticipate seldom occurs; what we least expected usually happens.

> —Benjamin Disraeli [7]

It's easy to be wise when you're not involved.

> —Unknown [7]

A crisis is when you can't say "let's forget the whole thing."

> —Ferguson's Precept [1]

Don't be afraid to take a big step if one is indicated You can't cross a chasm in two small jumps.

> —David Lloyd George [2]

Don't be afraid to go out on a limb—that's where the fruit is.

> —Unknown [2]

Security is mostly a superstition. It does not exist in nature. Life is either a daring adventure or nothing.

> —Helen Keller [2]

Far better it is to dare mighty things, to win glorious triumphs, even though checkered by failure, than to take rank with those poor spirits who neither enjoy much nor suffer much, because they live in the gray twilight that knows neither victory nor defeat.

> —Theodore Roosevelt [7]
> Speech to the Hamilton Club
> Chicago, April 10, 1899

In a surplus labor economy, the squeaking wheel does not get the grease; it gets replaced.
                    —Miller's Maxim [1]

It is not because things are difficult that we do not dare; it is because we do not dare that they are difficult.
                    —Seneca [7]

It wasn't raining when Noah built the ark.
                    —Howard Ruff [2]

Only those who risk going too far can possibly find out how far one can go.
                    —T.S. Eliot [2]

If you play not to lose, you lose. To get great ideas, breakthroughs, and innovation, you must accept, even embrace mistakes and, if managing others, provide an environment where it is perfectly safe to make mistakes. A key managerial skill is knowing when it is best to settle for less than perfection.
                    —Dan S. Kennedy [2]

Either you decide to stay in the shallow end of the pool or you go out in the ocean.
                    —Christopher Reeve [2]

Without courage, all other virtues lose their meaning.
                    —Winston Churchill [20]

There is no security in this life, only opportunity.
                    —Douglas MacArthur [20]

It's one thing to stick your neck out for a person, but when you stick your neck out for a system, it's just a waste of neck.
                    —Kathryn Hargrove [7]

STRESS, PRESSURE

Things get worse under pressure.
                    —Murphy's Law of
                        Thermodynamics [1]

Urgency varies inversely with importance.
                    —Frothingham's Fourth Law [1]

If you can keep your head when all about you are losing theirs, then
you obviously don't understand the problem.
                    —Evans's Law [1]

So much of what we call management consists of making it difficult
for people to work.
                    —Peter Drucker [2]

Wise people learn to tolerate only productive anxiety in themselves.
They make tension work for them instead of against them. Their ag-
gressiveness is outgoing and initiating, not hostile or arrogant.
                    —Unknown [2]

Carrying your cares to bed is like sleeping with a pack on your back.
                    —Not Attributed [2]

Discontent is the penalty we pay for being race horses instead of cows.
                    —Not Attributed [2]

I've never been satisfied with anything we've ever built. I've felt that
dissatisfaction is the basis of progress. When we become satisfied in
business, we become obsolete.
                    —J. Willard Marriott, Sr. [2]

There are two kinds of discontent, bad and good. The good kind will
motivate work. The bad kind will result in inactivity.
                    —Not Attributed [2]

You will never be the person you can be if pressure, tension, and discipline are taken out of your life.
—Dr. James G. Bilkey [2]

If you make the carrot too sweet and the load too light, then the business loses money and the cart grinds to a halt.
—Unknown [7]

Worry is a misuse of the imagination.
—Mary Crowley [7]

One of the manifestations of a poor self-image is someone who can't take any kidding.
—Unknown [7]

Frustration is not having anyone to blame but yourself.
—Not attributed [2]

The best defensive strategy is the courage to attack yourself.
—Al Ries and Jack Trout [11]

The psychic task that people can and must set for themselves is not to feel secure but to be able to tolerate insecurity.
—Erich Fromm [2]

Be thankful for your problems. If they were less difficult, someone with less ability might have your job.
—Not attributed [2]

No great advance has ever been made in science, politics, or religion without controversy.
—Lyman Beecher [2]
American clergyman

Life is either a tightrope or a feather bed. Give me the tightrope.
—Edith Wharton [2]

Peace comes not from the absence of conflict in life, but from the ability to cope with it.

—Not attributed [2]

I think every person faces challenges in his or her life, obstacles that they have to overcome to get where they want to be. Any successful person has failed somewhere along the line. It is never a clean ride.

—Tyrone "Muggsy" Bogues [2]
(Shortest professional basketball
player in the world)

The street to obscurity is paved with athletes who performed great feats before friendly crowds. Greatness in major league sports is the ability to win in a stadium filled with people who are pulling for you to lose.

—George Allen [2]

The unexpected always happens.

—Laurence J. Peter [2]

In spite of warnings, nothing much happens until the status quo becomes more painful than change.

—Laurence J. Peter [2]

There are no gains without pains.

—Adlai Stevenson [2]

Do what you are afraid to do.

—Mary Emerson [2]
(Aunt of Ralph Waldo Emerson)

You stand on a fulcrum between fear and faith—fear at your back, faith in front of you. Which way will you lean?

—Tom Hanks [7]
(2011 Yale University
commencement address)

SYSTEMS THINKING

A human being should be able to change a diaper, plan an invasion, butcher a hog, conn a ship, design a building, write a sonnet, balance accounts, build a wall, set a bone, comfort the dying, take orders, give orders, cooperate, act alone, solve equations, analyze a new problem, pitch manure, program a computer, cook a tasty meal, fight efficiently, die gallantly. Specialization is for insects.
—Lazarus Long [3]

The number of minor illnesses among the employees is inversely proportional to the health of the organization.
—Johnson's Law [1]

The chief cause of problems is solutions.
—Sevareid's Law [1]

In our haste to deal with the things that are wrong, let us not upset the things that are right.
—Not attributed [2]

Never test for an error condition you don't know how to handle.
—Steinbach's Guideline for
Systems Programming [1]

It is a simple thing to make things complex, but a complex task to make them simple.
—Meyer's Law [1]

Disorder expands proportionately to the tolerance for it.
—Welwood's Axiom [1]

In about five years there will be two types of CEOs; those who think globally and those who are unemployed.
—Peter Drucker [2]

There is chaos under heaven, and the situation is excellent.
—Mao Tze-Tung (attributed) [7]

The understanding of systems never lies in the system.
—Russell Ackoff [7]

Profound knowledge must come from outside the system and by invitation.
—W. E. Deming [7]

Predicting the future is easy compared with figuring out what's going on now.
—Unknown [7]

We trained very hard. But it seemed that every time we were beginning to form into teams, we would be reorganized. I was to learn later in life that we tend to meet any new situation by reorganizing. And what a wonderful method it can be for creating the illusion of progress while producing confusion, inefficiency, and demoralization.
—Charlton Ogburn, Jr. [21]
1911-1998

The system is not the sum of its parts, it is the product of the interaction of those parts.
—Russell Ackoff [27]

THINKING

When two people agree on everything, one of them is doing all the thinking.
—Not attributed [2]

If the assumptions are wrong, the conclusions aren't likely to be very good.
—Burns's Balance [4]

The narrower the mind, the broader the statement.
—Ted Cook [2]

The accommodation of so-called "traditional thinking" to new ideas evolves through three stages. The first is, "It can't possibly be true." In

the second it becomes, "Well, if it's true, it's not very important." The final stage is, "Well, we've known it all along."
—Unknown [7]

The significant problems we face cannot be solved at the same level of thinking we were at when we created them.
—Albert Einstein [12]

Info, info everywhere, but no one stops to think.
—H. Krantzberg [2]

It is remarkable to what lengths people will go to avoid thought.
—Thomas Edison [2]

The mind is a bit like a garden. If it isn't fed and cultivated, weeds will take over.
—Erving G. Hall [2]

Consider nothing impossible. Then treat all possibilities as probabilities.
—David Copperfield [2]

Thinking is the hardest work there is, which is the probable reason why so few engage in it.
—Henry Ford [2]

E
XAM
INE YOUR
ASSUMPTIONS
—Not attributed [2]

Research is what I'm doing when I don't know what I'm doing.
—Wernher von Braun [2]

No problem can withstand the assault of sustained thinking.
—Voltaire [7]

Rules are for when thinking stops.
—H. Dean Mallory [2]

Definition of *assumption:* The first sign of an impending disaster.
—Joe Heuer [2]

When you rule your mind, you rule your world. When you choose your thoughts, you choose results.
—Imelda Shanklin [2]

In all affairs it's a healthy thing now and then to hang a question mark on the things you have long taken for granted.
—Bertrand Russell [7]

Nothing pains some people more than having to think.
—Martin Luther King [20]

If everybody is thinking alike, then somebody isn't thinking.
—George S. Patton, Jr. [20]

The real problem is not whether machines think but whether men do.
—B.F. Skinner [7]

Five percent of the people think, ten percent of the people think that they think, and eighty-five percent would rather die than think.
—Thomas Edison [7]

TIMING

A powerful factor in success is a sense of timing. Every successful person I have ever known has had it—actor, businessman, writer, or politician. It is that instinct or ability to sense and seize the right moment without wavering or playing it safe. Without it many gifted people flicker brilliantly and briefly, then fade into oblivion in spite of their undoubted talents.
—Moss Hart [2]

WINNING AND LOSING

I don't like to lose, and that isn't so much because it is just a football game, but because the defeat means the failure to reach your objective. The trouble in American life today, in business as well as sports, is that too many people are afraid of competition. The result is that in some circles people have come to sneer at success if it costs hard work and training and sacrifice.

—Knute Rockne [2]

The race is not always to the swift, nor the battle to the strong—but that's the way to bet.

—Damon Runyon [2]

One very important ingredient of success is a good, wide-awake, persistent, tireless enemy.

—Not Attributed [2]

I don't know the formula for success, but I know the formula for failure—trying to please everybody.

—Todd Bozeman [7]
U. of California Basketball Coach

The difference between playing to win and playing not to lose is often the difference between success and mediocrity.

—Not attributed [2]

All things are difficult before they are easy . . . but doesn't that make your accomplishments more rewarding?

—Not Attributed [13]

In any field where there are a lot of skilled, highly trained competitors, nobody is twice as good—or even half as good—as everyone else. You don't have to be. A five or ten percent advantage will put you far ahead of the pack.

—Executive Speechwriter
Newsletter [2]

You have to be either first, best, or different.

—Loretta Lynn [2]

Competition is eternal. There is no such thing as winning. There is no end to the game. Even if you compete and win today, you must compete and win tomorrow.

> —Kuniuasu Sakai [2]
> Chairman, Taiyc Kogyo

The secret of all victory lies in the organization of the non-obvious.

> —Oswald Spengle: [2]

Those who win every battle are not really really skillful—those who render others' armies helpless without fighting are the best of all.

> —Sun Tzu [5]

If you know others and know yourself, you will not be imperiled in a hundred battles.

> —Sun Tzu [5]

Making armies able to take on opponents without being defeated is a matter of unorthodox and orthodox methods.

> —Sun Tzu [5]

To unfailingly take what you attack, attack where there is no defense.

> —Sun Tzu [5]

Accept the challenges, so that you may feel the exhilaration of victory.

> —Gen. George S. Patton [2]

No business opportunity is ever lost. If you fumble it, your competitor will find it.

> —Not attributed [2]

The three most important questions all winners ask themselves:

1. What do I want?
2. How am I going to get it?
3. When am I going to do something about it?

> —Mark Gibson [2]

THE SECRET TO SUCCESS: "Get to work early. Work late. Strike oil."
—John D. Rockefeller [2]

Success is not forever, and failure isn't fatal.
—Ken Blanchard [17]

The things that come to those who wait will be the things discarded by those who got there first.
—Not attributed [7]

Losers whine about doing their best. Winners go home and screw the prom queen.
—John Patrick Mason
(*The Rock*) [29]

Winning is a habit. Unfortunately, so is losing.
—Vince Lombardi [20]

AND FINALLY . . .

All the good maxims have been written. It remains to put them into practice.
—Blaise Pascal [2]

REFERENCES

1. Bloch, Arthur, **Murphy's Law Calendar**, Price Stern Sloan, Inc., 360 North La Cienega Boulevard, Los Angeles CA 90048, 1987.
2. **Bits and Pieces**, The Economic Press, Fairfield, NJ.
3. Heinlein, Robert A., **Time Enough for Love**, G.P. Putnam's Sons, New York, NY, 1973.
4. Dickson, Paul, **The Official Rules**, Dell Publishing Co., Inc., New York, NY, 1978.
5. Sun Tzu, **The Art of War** (translated by Thomas Cleary), Boston: Shambahala Publications, 1988.
6. Machiavelli, Niccolò, **The Prince**, New York: Quality Paperback Book Club, 1992.
7. Source unknown.
8. Conlin, Joseph R., **The Morrow Book of Quotations in American History**, William Morrow & Co., Inc., New York, 1984.
9. Heider, John, **The Tao of Leadership**, Bantam Books, New York, 1985.
10. O'Rourke, P.J., **Parliament of Whores.** New York: Vintage Books, 1991.
11. Thomsett, Michael C. **A Treasury of Business Quotations**. New York: Ballantine Books, 1990.
12. Covey, Steven R., **The Seven Habits of Highly Effective People**. New York: Fireside/Simon & Shuster, 1990.
13. Lynch, Tom. **Fun With Watercolor III**. Delray Beach, FL: Art is Fun, Inc., 1993.
14. Peters, Tom. **The Tom Peters Seminar**. New York: Vintage Books. 1994.
15. Kotter, John F. **Leading Change**. Cambridge, MA: Harvard Business School Press.
16. Sheehan, Neil. **A Bright Shining Lie**. NY: Vintage Books (Random House), 1988.
17. Blanchard, Ken. **The Heart of A Leader.** NY: Honor Books, 1998.
18. Senge, Peter. **The Fifth Discipline.** NY: Doubleday, 1990.
19. http://www.thinkexist.com/quotes/
20. Anderson, Peggy (compiled by). **Great Quotes from Great Leaders**. Franklin Lakes, NJ: Career Press, 1997.
21. http://quotes.liberty-tree.ca/quote_blog/Gaius.Petronius.Arbiter. Quote.7108

22. Commencement remarks, Chancellor Robert Holub, University of Massachusetts-Amherst (2009)
23. http://www.quotationspage.com/quotes/John_Ruskin/
24. http://www.quotationspage.com/quotes/Longfellow
25. Drucker, Peter. *Management: Tasks, Responsibilities, Practices.* NY: Harper-Collins. (1973)
26. Miyamoto, Musashi. *A Book of Five Rings.* (1645)
27. The Learning and Legacy of Dr. Deming (1994)
28. Bonner, Bill. *Diary of a Rogue Economist*, April 12, 2013.
29. *The Rock* (1996), Hollywood Pictures, Don Simpson/Jerry Bruckheimer Films.
30. *Chips Ahoy* (US Navy Magazine), July 1986.
31. *Kate and Leopold* (2001), Konrad Pictures, Miramax Films.
32. Hock, Dee W. *The Birth of the Chaordic Century*, Extension Leadership Conference, Washington, D.C., March 11, 1996.
33. http://www.grunt.com/corps/scuttlebutt/marine-corps-stories/col-mike-lowes-speech-at-quantico/
34. http://www.brainyquote.com/quotes/quotes/a/arthurgold170680.html#UI6fae2MYzgzzR6x.99
35. http://www.brainyquote.com/quotes/quotes/b/billgates122131.html
36. Richards, Chet. *Certain to Win: The Strategy of John Boyd, Applied to Business.* Xlibris (2004)
37. http://www.searchquotes.com/quotation/It_is_ridiculous_for_any_man_to_criticize_the_works_of_another_if_he_has_not_distinguished_himself_b/35688/

QUOTATIONS BY AUTHOR

RUSSELL ACKOFF
The system is not the sum of its parts, it is the product of the interaction of those parts.

The understanding of systems never lies in the system.

MUHAMMAD ALI
The fight is won or lost far away from witnesses—behind the lines, in the gym, and out there on the road, long before I dance under those lights.

JOHN R. BOYD
People, ideas, technology—in that order!

Bad news is the only kind that will do you any good.

PAUL "BEAR" BRYANT
The first time you quit, it's hard. The second time, it gets easier. The third time, you don't even have to think about it.

I'm just a plowhand from Arkansas, but I have learned how to hold a team together. How to lift some men up, how to calm down others, until finally they've got one heartbeat together, a team. There's just three things I'd ever say:

- If anything goes bad, I did it.
- If anything goes semi-good, then we did it.
- If anything goes real good, then you did it.

That's all it takes to get people to win football games for you.

ANDREW CARNEGIE
No man will make a great leader who wants to do it all himself, or to get all the credit for doing it.

There is no use whatever in trying to help people who do not help themselves. You cannot push anyone up a ladder unless he is willing to climb himself.

WINSTON CHURCHILL
Man will occasionally stumble over the truth, but most of the time he will pick himself up and continue on.

A fanatic is one who can't change his mind and won't change the subject.

Dogs look up to you; cats look down on you; pigs treat you as an equal.

The farther back you can look, the farther forward you are likely to see.

You Americans will always do the right thing, after you exhaust all other possibilities.

The most essential qualification for a politician is the ability to foretell what will happen tomorrow, next month, and next year—and to explain afterward why it did not happen.

Any 20-year-old who isn't a liberal doesn't have a heart, and any 40-year-old who isn't a conservative doesn't have a brain.

Capitalism's problem is the uneven distribution of wealth, while socialism's virtue is the even distribution of misery.

There are two places where socialism will work: In heaven, where it is not needed, and in Hell, where they already have it.

Without courage, all other virtues lose their meaning.

CALVIN COOLIDGE
Nothing in this world can take the place of persistence. Talent will not; nothing is more common than unsuccessful men with talent. Genius will not; unrewarded genius is almost a proverb. Education will not; the world is full of educated derelicts. Persistence and determination alone are omnipotent. The slogan "press on" has solved and always will solve the problems of the human race.

STEVEN COVEY
Anything less than a conscious commitment to the important is an unconscious commitment to the unimportant.

DANIEL DEFOE
It is better to have a lion at the head of an army of sheep, than a sheep at the head of an army of lions.

W. EDWARDS DEMING
It is not necessary to change; survival is not mandatory.

The penalty for ignorance is you get beat up.

How many families have a merit system to measure one child against another? Why should merit systems in the work place do any more to engender team cooperation?

Work under a master. Nothing takes the place of working under a master. Get a job where there is one, travel with him, watch what he does.

One who learns a thing as a skill cannot easily change.

There is nothing in a Japanese car that wasn't in an American car first. They just did it better. We smother innovation with the merit system.

Competition should be directed toward doing a better job, not toward getting a bigger share of the market. Do the first, and the second will take care of itself.

Profound knowledge must come from outside the system and by invitation.

PETER DRUCKER
There is one thing all boards have in common, regardless of their legal position. They do not function.

Information technology so far may well have done serious damage to management, because it is so good at getting additional information of the wrong kind.

Management is not being brilliant. Management is being conscientious. Beware the genius manager. Management is doing a very few simple things and doing them well.

Effectiveness is doing the RIGHT things; efficiency is doing things RIGHT. Productivity is doing the RIGHT things RIGHT.

My greatest strength as a consultant is to be ignorant and ask a few questions.

The only things that evolve by themselves in an organization are disorder, friction, and malperformance.

Long-range planning does not deal with future decisions, but with the future of present decisions.

So much of what we call management consists of making it difficult for people to work.

In about five years there will be two types of CEOs; those who think globally and those who are unemployed.

THOMAS EDISON
I have not failed 10,000 times. I have successfully found 10,000 ways that will not work.

It is remarkable to what lengths people will go to avoid thought.

Five percent of the people think, ten percent of the people think that they think, and eighty-five percent would rather die than think.

ALBERT EINSTEIN
Weakness of attitude becomes weakness of character.

Any intelligent fool can make things bigger and more complex. It takes a touch of genius—and a lot of courage—to move in the opposite direction.

Great spirits have always encountered violent opposition from mediocre minds.

The only thing that interferes with my learning is my education.

Education is what remains after one has forgotten what one has learned in school.

When a man sits with a pretty girl for an hour, it seems like a minute. But let him sit on a hot stove for a minute—and it's longer than any hour. That's relativity.

I have little patience with scientists who take a board of wood, look for its thinnest part, and drill a great number of holes where drilling is easy.

Not everything that can be counted counts, and not everything that counts can be counted.

The significant problems we face cannot be solved at the same level of thinking we were at when we created them.

DWIGHT D. EISENHOWER
In order to be a leader, a man must have followers. And to have followers, a man must have their confidence. Hence the supreme quality for a leader is unquestionably integrity. Without it, no real success is possible, no matter whether it is on a section gang, on a football field, in an army, or in an office. If a man's associates find him guilty of phoniness, if they find that he lacks forthright integrity, he will fail. His teachings and actions must square with each other. The first great need, therefore, is integrity and high purpose.

I would rather try to persuade a man to go along, because once I have persuaded him, he will stick. If I scare him, he will stay just as long as he is scared, and then he is gone.

A people that values its privileges above its principles soon loses both.

RALPH WALDO EMERSON

Do not go where the path may lead. Go instead where there is no path and leave a trail.

What you are shouts so loudly in my ears I cannot hear what you say.

Don't waste time in doubts and fears; spend yourself in the work before you, well assured that the right performance of this hour's duties will be the best preparation for the hours or ages that follow it.

Common sense is genius dressed up in its working clothes.

Whoso would be a man must be a nonconformist. Nothing is at last sacred but the integrity of the mind.

HENRY FORD

Failure is simply the opportunity to begin again more intelligently.

Don't find fault. Find a remedy.

Thinking is the hardest work there is, which is the probable reason why so few engage in it.

Enthusiasm is at the bottom of all progress. With it, there is accomplishment. Without it there are only alibis.

If there is any one secret of success, it lies in the ability to get the other person's point of view and see things from his angle as well as your own.

There is one rule for industrialists and that is: make the best quality of goods possible at the lowest possible cost, paying the highest wages possible.

I'm looking for a lot of men with an infinite capacity for not knowing what can't be done.

BENJAMIN FRANKLIN
Wise men don't need advice. Fools won't take it.

He that cannot obey, cannot command.

If you would persuade, you must appeal to interest rather than intellect.

He that lives upon hope dies farting.

MOHANDAS K. GANDHI
If I believe I cannot do something, it makes me incapable of doing it. But when I believe I can, then I acquire the ability to do it, even if I did not have the ability in the beginning.

In my humble opinion, noncooperation with evil is as much a duty as cooperation with good.

DEE HOCK
Everything has both intended and unintended consequences. The intended consequences may or may not happen. The unintended consequences always do. (The Sheep's First Law of the Universe)

Simple, clear purpose and principles give rise to complex, intelligent behavior. Complex rules and regulations give rise to simple, stupid behavior. (The Sheep's Second Law of the Universe)

Everything is its opposite, particularly competition and cooperation. Neither can rise to its highest potential unless seamlessly blended with the other. Either without the other swiftly becomes dangerous and destructive. (The Sheep's Third Law of the Universe)

The problem is never how to get new, innovative thoughts into your mind, but how to get old ones out.

ALDOUS HUXLEY
Facts do not cease to exist because they are ignored.

HELEN KELLER
Security is mostly a superstition. It does not exist in nature. Life is either a daring adventure or nothing.

JOHN F. KENNEDY
A man does what he must—in spite of personal consequences, in spite of obstacles and dangers and pressures—and that is the basis of all human morality.

Forgive your enemies, but never forget their names.

MARTIN LUTHER KING, JR.
The height of your accomplishments will equal the depth of your convictions.

Nothing pains some people more than having to think.

VINCE LOMBARDI
The difference between a successful person and others is not a lack of strength, not a lack of knowledge, but rather a lack of will.

Winning is a habit. Unfortunately, so is losing.

JOHN STUART MILL
A man who has nothing for which he is willing to fight, nothing he cares about more than his own personal safety, is a miserable creature who has no chance of being free, unless made and kept so by the exertions of better men than himself.

FRIEDRICH NIETZSCHE
By losing your goal, you have lost your way.

THOMAS PAINE
The harder the conflict, the more glorious the triumph. What we obtain cheap, we esteem to lightly; 'tis dearness only that gives everything its value.

Public money ought to be touched with the most scrupulous conscientiousness of honor. It is not the product of riches only, but of the hard earnings of labor and poverty. It is drawn even from the bitterness of want and misery. Not a beggar passes, or perishes in the streets, whose mite is not in that mass.

GEORGE S. PATTON, JR.
All my life I've been shot at. Often by the enemy.

If you tell people where to go, but not how to get there, you'll be amazed at the results.

If a man has done his best, what else is there?

Accept the challenges, so that you may feel the exhilaration of victory.

PLATO
We can easily forgive a child who is afraid of the dark; the real tragedy of life is when men are afraid of the light.

The beginning is the most important part of the work.

LAURENCE J. PETER

TOP 10 EXCUSES

1. I thought it was in the mail.
2. I'm so busy I haven't gotten around to it.
3. I didn't know you were in a hurry for it.
4. You'll have to wait until the supervisor returns.
5. I'm waiting for an OK.
6. That's their job—not mine.
7. No one told me to go ahead.
8. That's not my department.
9. That's the way it's always done here.
10. Just as soon as it clears the review board, we'll process your application.

The unexpected always happens.

In spite of warnings, nothing much happens until the status quo becomes more painful than change.

TOM PETERS
Powerlessness is a state of mind. If you THINK you're powerless, you ARE.

Obsession doesn't guarantee success. On the other hand, a lack of obsession does guarantee failure.

THEODORE ROOSEVELT
In a moment of decision, the best thing you can do is the right thing to do. The worst thing you can do is nothing.

The best executive is the one who has enough sense to pick good people to do what he wants done, and self-restraint enough to keep from meddling with them while they do it.

Ninety percent of the work in this country is done by people who don't feel well.

Far better it is to dare mighty things, to win glorious triumphs, even though checkered by failure, than to take rank with those poor spirits who neither enjoy much nor suffer much, because they live in the gray twilight that knows neither victory nor defeat.

JOHN RUSKIN
Quality is never an accident; it is always the result of intelligent effort.

There is scarcely anything in the world that some man cannot make a little worse, and sell a little more cheaply. The person who buys on price alone is this man's lawful prey.

ALBERT SCHWEITZER
Man must cease attributing his problems to his environment and learn again to exercise his will—his personal responsibility.

BOOKER T. WASHINGTON
I think I began learning long ago that those who are happiest are those who do the most for others.

Success is to be measured not so much by the position that one has reached in life as by the obstacles that one has overcome while trying to succeed.

GEORGE WASHINGTON
My observation is that whenever one person is found adequate to the discharge of a duty by close application thereto, it is worse executed by two persons, and scarcely done at all if three or more are employed therein.

JOHN WOODEN
Failure is not fatal, but failure to change might be.

Ability may get you to the top, but it takes character to keep you there.

It's what you learn after you know it all that counts.

Failure to prepare is preparing to fail.

Israel

An Artist's Journey through the Holy Land

Copies of this book are available at:

IngridWrightFineArt.com
Amazon.com

Please note:
All of the artwork in *Israel: An Artist's Journey Through the Holy Land* is created by Dr. Ingrid Wright and is protected by copyright laws of the United States.

Acknowledgments

JAY for editing and his loving support.

JOAN for her godly vision & boundless energy.

CHARITY for taking me from concept to finished book in a very short time.

CAROL for bringing the passion I had for this book to life.

ISRAEL for its welcoming spirit & visual inspiration.

Dedication

This book is dedicated to:

My wonderful husband, my travel partner and best friend, Jay.

Our children, Brian and Julie.

Thank you all for every journey we are blessed to enjoy together.

Endorsements

When you visit Israel, God will meet with you in a personal way. For Ingrid, God encountered her in a very special way and inspired her to create this book.

It was an honor to host Ingrid and her husband, Jay, on this tour.

I encourage you to let God speak to you also through these drawings and through the inspired words.

Bo Sander
Executive Director
Biblical Journeys

Dr. Ingrid is a dear friend and one of the most positive people I know. Her love for God and desire to see people closer to Him shines through in everything she does.

Jeremy and Jenifer Kraus,
Founders of Thrive Rescue and
Thrive Justice School

Through her paintings, Ingrid's unique style and talent takes us firsthand to the inspiring and historically significant locations in the Holy Land. If you are traveling to Israel, Ingrid's book becomes your personal journal capturing each special location.

Rick Green
Author, Speaker, & former Texas Legislator

Table of Contents

Foreword

I love Israel and I love art. In *Israel, An Artist's Journey Through the Holy Land*, Dr. Ingrid Wright has combined her love of the Holy Land with beautiful watercolor drawings and the scripture to produce an incredible journal. It can be used as a journal for those visiting Israel as you travel around the country or it can be used as a place to record prayerful insights that deal with Israel. I believe this work will be a great blessing to you!

Joan Hunter
Author/Speaker/Evangelist
Joan Hunter Ministries
www.joanhunter.org

Introduction

"Please return to your seats and fasten your seat belts, as we begin our descent into Tel Aviv. We will be landing shortly." The captain's words brought a wave of energy and excitement to us, because our holy land tour was about to officially begin!

Israel is a country so abundant in biblical history with its roots encompassing the birth of Christianity.

Every stop on our tour took us to yet another exciting place that suddenly made the well-known Bible stories come to life. At each new location, God helped me to capture these biblical moments visually on paper with watercolor paintings.

On March 17, 2017, the Lord told me to assemble seventeen of these paintings into a collection of highlights from that recent trip to Israel. Joan Hunter encouraged, guided & collaborated with me in the production of this project. She also told me that the number "17" means complete victory in overcoming the enemy. Praise God!

Be blessed as you embark on this artistic journey and experience Israel's rich heritage. Have a fun trip!

Ingrid

Sea of Galilee

Jesus feeds the five thousand.

> *"Jesus then took the loaves, gave thanks, and distributed to those who were seated as much as they wanted. He did the same with the fish."* – John 6:11

Jesus calls his first disciples.

> *"Come, follow me," Jesus said, "and I will send you out to fish for people."* – Mark 1:17

Jesus walks on water.

> *"Shortly before dawn Jesus went out to them walking on the lake."* – Matthew14:25

Mount of Beatitudes - Site of the Sermon on the Mount

> *"Now when Jesus saw the crowds, He went up on a mountainside and sat down. His disciples came to Him and He began to teach them."* – Matthew 5:1-2

Magdala

Home of Mary Magdalene who helped to fund Jesus' ministry
(Luke 8:4-15)

"These women were helping to support them
out of their own means." – Luke 8:3

Mount Carmel

Elijah defeated the prophets of Baal.

(1 Kings 18:16-46)

> *"When all the people saw this, they fell prostrate and*
> *cried, "The Lord – He is God! The Lord – He is God!"*
> *–1 Kings 18:39–*

Baptism in the Jordan River

The location where John baptized Jesus

(Matt 3:13-17, Luke 3:21-22, John 3:26)

> *"At that time Jesus came from Nazareth in Galilee and was baptized by John in the Jordan."*
> –Mark 1:9–

The Dead Sea Float

Lot's wife turned to a pillar of salt.

*"But Lot's wife looked back, and she became
a pillar of salt." – Genesis 19:26*

Masada – (Hebrew for "fortress")

The site where more than 900 Jews committed mass suicide rather than surrender to the Roman army. Today, Israeli soldiers declare, "Masada shall not fall again!"

Western Wall

Sacred place of prayer near the Holy of Holies

(Nehemiah 2:5, Psalms 122:2)

"Then the people of the Lord went down to the city gates."
–Judges 5:11–

The Holy of Holies

Sacred place where the High Priest convened with God once a year (Exodus 26:33-34, 2 Chronicles 3:1-14)

*"Behind the second curtain was a room called the
Most Holy Place." – Hebrews 9:3*

Healing Pools at Bethesda

Jesus healed the man that came to Him.

(John 5:1-9)

> *"Then Jesus said to him, "Get up! Pick up your mat and walk." – John 5:8*

The Last Supper in the Upper Room

Jesus' last meal with His disciples prior to His arrest

(Matthew 26:17-30, Mark 14:12-26, Luke 22:7-39, John 13:1-17:26)

"He will show you a large room upstairs, all furnished.
Make preparations there." – Luke 22:12

Garden of Gethsemane

Jesus prayed here the night before His arrest.

(Mark 14:32-42, Luke 22:40-46)

> *"Then Jesus went with His disciples to a place called Gethsemane, and He said to them, "sit here while I go over there and pray." – Matthew 26:36*

Via Dolorosa

Jesus' path from prison to crucifixion

(Matthew 27:33-44, Mark 15:16-32)

> *"Carrying His own cross, He went out to the place of the skull (Golgotha). There they crucified Him, and with Him two others – one on each side and Jesus in the middle."*
> –John 19:17-18–

Garden Tomb

The site of Jesus' burial and resurrection

(John 19:38-42, Matthew 27:57-61, Mark 15:42-47, Luke 23:50-56)

> *"At the place where Jesus was crucified, there was a garden, and in the garden a new tomb, in which no one had ever been laid…they laid Jesus there."*
> –John 19:41–

Mediterranean Sea at Joppa

One of the oldest ports in the world

Solomon (2 Chronicles 2:16), Jonah (Jonah 1:3) & Peter (Acts 9:36) all spent time here.

"She opened her eyes, and seeing Peter she sat up."
– Acts 9:40–

Roman Aqueduct

The Aqueduct brought running water to Israel.

"I will turn the desert into pools of water."
– Isaiah 41:18–

Shiloh

Hannah cried out to God for a son.

(1 Samuel 1:9-19)

> *"And she made a vow, saying, "Lord Almighty,…*
> *remember me…give me a son, then I will give him to the*
> *Lord for all the days of his life…" – 1 Samuel 1:11*

Bethlehem

Jesus was born.

(Luke 2:15, John 7:42)

> *"Today in the Town of David a Savior has been born;*
> *He is the Messiah, the Lord." – Luke 2:11*

INGRIDWRIGHTFINEART.COM

Traveling inspires Ingrid's passion to capture "God's beauty around us" in her artwork. Born and raised in San Francisco, Ingrid has a Bachelor's Degree in Chemistry from SF State University and graduated from UOP Dental School in 1982.

Along with building a very successful dental practice, Ingrid has also enjoyed a career as a fashion model, TV commercial spokesperson, martial arts instructor, and her "higher calling" as a wife and mother.

Her motto is: "It's never too late to start something new and exciting!" Ingrid became passionate in 2001 about creating fine art, which has been featured at fine art shows and in private collections throughout the US, Canada, Australia and Europe.

Website: IngridWrightFineArt.com •Twitter: @DrIngridWright

Two More Books from Dr. Ingrid Wright

Daily Whispers from God

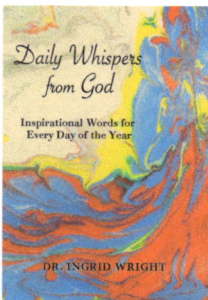

Inspirational Words for Every Day of the Year, showcases a monthly beautiful black and white ink painting by Dr. Wright, daily prophetic words, scriptures, and space to journal insights.

Nature One Evening

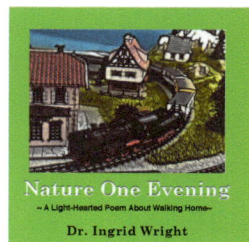

A Light-hearted poem about walking home. Dr. Ingrid Wright has written a wonderful poem and illustrated it with her beautiful artwork, for all ages to enjoy.